'Occupy Wall Street,' To What End?

New Economy Solutions
From an Ancient Source

By L. (EliYahu) Hefley

Edition 1, © 2011

Published by L. (EliYahu) Hefley

www.createspace.com/3732661
ISBN-13: 978-1467985178
ISBN-10: 1467985171

Thank you, Father,
For Your mercy, wisdom and love.

Table of Contents

'Occupy Wall Street,' To What End?

There are a lot of people who are fed up with our country, who have lost their jobs and are protesting against Wall Street. 'Occupy Wall Street' was born out of the frustration of the working class, who has been impoverished. They don't know what the solution is exactly. But they know that the greed of the superrich has brought this nation to its knees, making them jobless and their families homeless. And they know that if a solution does not present itself, starvation and violence will only grow more widespread until the nation collapses completely. So what is the solution?

Politicians for the most part, looking to solve the problems of the economy and the deficit, both Republican and Democrat, simply want to throw money at the problem. Putting more money into government services or in tax cuts simply does not work. Even balancing the budget by cutting services will not work because it does not address the production problem. They say that their plan will provide jobs, but both parties have tried their plans and the economy is still in the pits. It is the work climate of our culture that is the problem. And money cannot fix this. We need to understand the problem and fix it at its root, not just throw money at it.

Some are proposing the tired old solution of Communism, since it is Free Enterprise that seems to be the cause of our current economic crisis. We understand that Free Enterprise does not work. Its greed is squeezing the life out of our country. Laissez-Faire, from the French for 'leave it alone,' refers to Free Enterprise, which is the policy that the Government should not interfere with the market. It is what has empowered the rich to legally steal from the poor. The income gap between the rich and the poor is ever widening, because of Laissez-Faire politics. Before government was invented, the rich were the powerful who could take from the poor by force.

Government was invented to protect the weak from the rich.

"We hold these Truths to be self-evident, that all Men are created equal, that they are endowed, by their Creator, with certain unalienable Rights, that among these are Life, Liberty, and the Pursuit of Happiness.--That to secure these Rights, Governments are instituted among Men, deriving their just Powers from the Consent of the Governed." Declaration of Independence

And yet today, the government protects the rich from the poor. This is because the rich use bribes, (called 'lobbying') to make the laws advantageous to them. Senator McCain has made a career of trying to defeat 'Soft Money,' as he calls it. But the bribes have prevailed.

"And you shall take no gift: for the gift blinds the wise, and perverts the words of the righteous." (Exodus 23:8)

The superrich bribe… I mean lobby, through the Republicans, while the not quite as rich, AKA the Mafia, lobby through the Democrats. Thus the rich agenda wins regardless of who wins the elections. And every year the rich are able to squeeze a little more out of the profits of the workers. What is the difference between the superrich and the Mafia? The theft that the superrich do has been legalized, because they give bigger bribes.

Laissez-Faire is in essence the policy of no government, where the 1% rich use their power to enslave the weak. And the 99% are fed up with it, and rightly so.

But Communism does not work either. We know this from history also. Both Russia and China have abandoned Communism because it does not work. The incentive for profit is what drives workers to produce more. Redistribution of income wealth destroys that incentive to produce more, and they ended up with bare shelves at the supermarket. So they instituted a mixture of Free Enterprise and Socialism. Proponents of Communism in the U.S. instituted Socialism here back in the thirties, called the 'New Deal.' And so we too have a mixture of Free Enterprise and Socialism. But this mixture provides us with the worst of both systems. The more you make, the more is taken from you, so the incentive to produce more by the common worker is lowered. And the superrich lend money to the poor who have to borrow to live, making the rich richer and the poor poorer. In a sense, we are a slave society, where the poor cater to the needs of the rich and get paid diddly-squat for their trouble.

The welfare system is supposed to be the remedy for this. But it is set up so that you lose all your benefits if you work. What advantage is there to get a part time job at minimum wage that will not pay the bills? It pays better to sit at home and have babies out of wedlock. As a result of Socialism, we have more people on the dole than our economy can support.

"You cannot solve a problem with the same mindset that created it." Albert Einstein

The problems of society are caused by the culture of that society, rather than being something that is inevitable. Therefore the answer to society's problems lies in changing the basic paradigms of our culture. One definition of insanity is doing the same thing over and over even though it fails each time. Our culture is insane and needs to be changed at its very root.

Two Types of Profit

We have been taught in school that there are only two economic options: The Left, which is Communism, and the Right which is Free Enterprise. And so we opt for a solution that is somewhere in the middle. But there is another solution. This solution is found in the dusty old pages of the Law of Moses. It provides specific laws that provide both the full profit motive and the protection of the poor from the rich.

The key to this solution is understanding that the profit motive, which is designed to motivate workers to produce more, also hides a second more sinister profit motive to make money from your money. If we separate these two types of profit, we can see where the problem comes in.

Obviously we want to motivate workers to produce more. And so we want to keep this profit motive alive. We do this by personal ownership. State property destroys ownership and with it the ownership of the profit from our work, which destroys the workers' motivation to work, and which killed Communism historically. The Bible guarantees personal ownership by the command, "Thou shalt not steal." So this sharing economy that we are proposing is not Communism. The state does not own anything.

It is the right to keep what you earn that motivates workers to work not only harder, but smarter. It keeps the workers focused on production, rather than just punching a time card, or complaining about their wages, or doing some easy work that does not contribute to production, like paperwork. This simple concept of personal ownership is the foundation of a good economy. Allowing workers to keep all the profit from their work motivates them to produce more.

"Each day you shall give him his wages, and not let the sun go down on it, for he is poor and has set his heart on it; lest he cry out against you to the Lord, and it be sin to you." (Deuteronomy 24:15)

But this other type of profit, making money from your money, is what makes the rich richer and the poor poorer. If the rich can leverage money away from the workers, then the wealth disparity will grow and grow. In this country the amount of income of the superrich is ridiculously higher than the income of the average worker, and that disparity is growing every year. And as that disparity grows, the motivation of the workers to work diminishes.

Making money from your money does not motivate people to work harder or smarter to produce things. It motivates people to figure out ways to use their money to leverage money out of those who have less of it. It focuses workers attention away from work and onto stealing.

The command to not steal means a lot more than our culture's concept of it. It also refers to things that we consider to be naturally legal. Whether a certain kind of stealing is legal or not, it is wrong, and it destroys the motivation to work. Just because a practice is longstanding does not make it right.

Taking a part of the profit from someone else's work is stealing, regardless of whether it is legal or not. If someone can legally steal from me, then why should I work hard? Why should I work so that others can steal and profit from my work? And with this reduction of the motive to work, comes the destruction of the economy. And because we embrace this idea of making money from our money, a type of theft, our economy is about to collapse.

Making Money From Your Money

What exactly does it mean to make money from your money? As an owner of capital, I can make money by investing my money in a bank that pays interest. The more money I have, the more money I make. This money that I make from interest is not from work. It is simply from the fact that I have more money than the guy who is paying the interest to borrow it. I am making this money without lifting a finger to produce a thing. I am not contributing to the economy by this, but rather I am taking a cut from the economy.

But I want to make money from my money, so that when I am old and can no longer work, I can still make money and survive. My money is my security. But who is ultimately paying this interest to me? It is the poor who do not have money who have to borrow money to survive. Thus I am taking money from the poor worker and paying myself because I have money. This makes the rich richer and the poor poorer. This use of interest is a legal form of stealing from the poor. In the Bible, interest is forbidden. It is called 'usury;' a word we never hear today.

"If you lend money to any of my people that is poor by you, you shall not be to him as an usurer, neither shall you put upon him usury." (Exodus 22:25)

And who are the poor that I am stealing from? They are the workers. When you steal from the poor by means of this 'usury,' you are de-motivating them from work, and destroying the economy that fuels the interest that you seek. You are killing the goose that is laying the golden egg.

But we do not want to give this up, because this is our security. So what I am proposing here is a complete paradigm shift of our economic culture. Our security must come from something other than our money. When money is no longer our security, making ridiculous piles of it at the expense of others will no longer be so important.

The form of security that I am proposing here is Exclusive Communities. The foundation of this type of security is that we share with our extended family, the community, because we want our community to succeed economically, so that it can share with us when we have need. We naturally do this within families. We are simply extending this to a larger group, so that our security can be larger.

The Bible has a law that requires people to lend to those in need without interest, if they have means to do so.

"If one of your brethren becomes poor, and falls into poverty among you, then you shall help him, like a stranger or a sojourner, that he may live with you. Take no usury or interest from him; but fear your God, that your brother may live with you. You shall not lend him your money for usury, nor lend him your food at a profit." (Leviticus 25:35-37)

Jesus reiterated this. "Whoever asks you, give to him. And he who wants to borrow from you, you should not refuse him." (Matthew 5:42)

This is done directly to people within your community. It does not apply to organizations, or even to government agencies, which skim a portion off the top. It applies to individuals in need in your community. These people are local people who live close enough to be friends.

This gives you control to designate who is in legitimate need. It provides what welfare intends without the government skimming off the top, or letting scammers dip into the fund. Welfare intends to get people back on their feet, but more often than not, they cannot fully reach the level where they can really make it on their own. Some piece of red tape stands between them some piece of the puzzle. So they become trapped in welfare. As a friend I am motivated to help this friend to get a skill and to help him until he gets his feet on the ground again. This builds our community, rather than constantly adding people who sponge off the system.

And because this is giving to friends in a community, no paperwork is necessary. Community insurance can be handled with little or no paperwork. Community taxes would require little or no paperwork. Instead of being choked by bureaucracy and paperwork everywhere you turn, most of it would go away, because most transaction would be from one trusted friend to another.

A tight community encourages everyone to pull their weight in the local work force. There used to be a great stigmatism against receiving a dole, decades ago. That was because we had to look into the face of those that were giving us charity, when we were not contributing. Now, many people feel the government owes them welfare. Many people feel that they are better than others if they can get more by cheating. This is a criminal thought process, which is born out of legalizing theft by the rich, and the breakup of the community.

When a community works face to face together, we no longer want to step on them to get ahead, because they are our friends. That same welfare cheater is keen to make the chores at home equal among members. Small communities that help each other face to face are the first step in this paradigm shift.

Below I will discuss how this type of community works in detail. But before I do, I want to discuss more of the issues associated with making money from our money. These issues will define the type of community that we will want to create.

Rent

Another way that the rich legally steal from the poor is rent.

"The land shall not be sold for ever: for the land is mine; for you are strangers and sojourners with me." (Leviticus 25:23)

It is against the Bible to foreclose on the basic necessities of the poor to make a living, not only because it is immoral, but also because it destroys the economy.

"If you ever take your neighbor's garment as a pledge, you shall return it to him before the sun goes down." (Exodus 22:26)

"No man shall take the lower or the upper millstone in pledge, for he takes one's living in pledge." (Deuteronomy 24:6)

You cannot take a person's ancestral home, or his last set of clothes, or his basic tools for his personal business. Only with these things can a person reasonably continue to make money to pay off his debts and contribute to the economy. Taking these basics from the poor destroys production, and thus the economy, which is exactly the cause of our economic crisis today. It is greed that crosses this line. It cuts off the nose to spite the face.

In the Bible, every citizen is in the military. (Numbers 1:2-3) Thus every citizen having paid for the freedom of that land deserves a little piece of that land. And so every veteran is given a small piece of land for his family permanently. Thus no citizen should be paying rent under that system.

If these homes are given to veterans only, then there is an incentive to join the military and help pay for the freedom of this land. In the Bible soldiers were not paid. Instead they served in a reserve status. Their families and communities supplied them when they away on maneuvers. (I Samuel 17:38-40) It was their land that was their pay for their service.

This also means that our wars should exclusively be for the purpose of protecting that land, not getting oil so that the superrich can make more money from their money. Back when I was in the Marines, I was briefed that our primary purpose in the Iraqi war was to secure oil, as if this was common knowledge. And yet that statement was never made publicly, by any politician in government. How can voters, vote intelligently, if much of our policies are secret from the public?

If our military was made up of local community militias, like the Second Amendment suggests, then we would have leverage over our war policies and could get un-propagandized information on governmental policies.

"A well regulated Militia, being necessary to the security of a free State, the right of the people to keep and bear Arms, shall not be infringed." The Second Amendment

How does rent allow the rich to make money from their money? Those that have money buy homes or apartments and rent to those who do not have money. The payment to the bank for the land, the building, the maintenance, the repairs and the interest comes from the renter, not the wealthy owner. The poor renter has paid a large portion of his pay from his work to the rich person for the privilege of buying an income making home, for the rich guy. After a number of years, the rich person has paid off the property and is now in a position to buy more property and make more money, while the poor worker owns nothing. And if he gets old and stops working, he will lose his home.

The Free Enterprise promoters counter that he should save his money and buy his own place. But if a large part of his income goes to rent, and his job pays little, then he will never have enough to save anything. Because this allows the rich to make more money on their money, it makes the rich richer and the poor poorer. And as the rich get richer, more and more of the poor are placed in a position where they can never save up for a home of their own.

Rent is based on feudalism and is designed to keep the king and the land owners in power. Lords thought that the workers owed them this because of their birth, which came from their ancestors who conquered the other guys. Today the rich think the workers owe them this because of their wealth, which came from their ancestors who somehow conquered the other guys. But was not our Constitution designed to throw off kings and feudalism?

Speaking of feudalism, the 'Peasant Revolt' of 1381 started because the peasants were being taxed by the landholders at a rate of 25%, the highest tax rate of the middle ages. Normally taxes were around 10% under feudalism. Our tax rate on the middle class is higher than that and yet we quietly abide this oppression. But that 25% also included their rent payment. Today, many workers pay 30% taxes, and then 50% for rent on top of that. That is 80% to the landholders. And we wonder why the workers have stopped working.

Our current solution is for the government to help people to get bigger loans. This is what has tempted the poor to buy a home that places his budget on a tight line. And when there is the slightest problem with their income, or expenses, they lose their home, because they have no buffer to work with. But the bank makes out, because it gets the interest that was paid, and the home, which it can sell at a profit. It is a profit to them because they stole it from some guy that lost his job. Helping the banks get more loans from the poor is not helping the poor. It is helping the rich bankers.

The only real remedy for this is the redistribution of land. This is not taking income from workers. It is giving ownership of homes and apartments to those who live in them, by taking them away from the rich who use these places to steal money from the workers. Because this is currently a legal means making money, it is a retirement strategy for many. Thus to implement this reform in fairness, some sort of transition plan should be used. But again the community must be the source of security, rather than money. But ultimately it will involve taking these rental homes and apartments from the wealthy, and giving them to the citizens who live there.

But the big losers in this transaction will be the banks who own the mortgages. When the properties are given to the occupants, the owners who are renting the properties should not also have to continue to pay the mortgage on the property. Instead the mortgages should be dissolved. Additionally those who own their own home, by means of a mortgage, should have their mortgages dissolved. It is hardly fair to give homes to renters, and not to those who own their own mortgage. But that is a good thing since banks are a primary source of interest theft.

Thomas Jefferson understood this, when he said, "Banking Establishments are more dangerous than standing armies."

The money taken from rental property owners for the most part is not money that they earned by work, but money that they stole by rent. And likewise the money taken from banks by dissolving mortgages is primarily money stolen by interest, not profit from work.

Our current bailout strategy is to have the government pay the banks directly or by helping people get mortgages. The government has no money. It is in debt up to its eyeballs. And it is giving money to banks, who own the whole country, and are renting it to the workers; legally stealing from them. What is wrong with that picture? But while the government has no money, it does have something else that could help us. It has the power to outlaw this type of theft called 'rent.' It is the purpose of the government to protect its workers from theft.

The word 'mortgage' comes from the Latin word for 'death.' It means a loan that you take till you die. But it really means the death of the golden goose. The economy is based on the work of workers. When you take the incentive for work away from the workers by taking most of their pay for rent or mortgage payments, you kill the economy eventually. Anyone who cannot make ends meet because too much of his pay goes to rent is going to be thinking about some other means of survival besides work. Many go on welfare. Others go to crime.

The crime rate in this country is higher than any other country in the world. One of the reasons for that is that crime pays better than work. It pays better because it is a way to steal from the rich and give to the poor. It also pays better because work pays so little, after the rich take their cut from the wages. If working means stealing from the poor to give to the rich through rent, then crime is the only alternative for many, hence the popularity of Robin Hood. Should they not reason that if it is ok for the rich to steal from them through rent, should it not also be ok for them to steal from the rich by burglary?

But again both types of theft take the profit from the worker and de-motivate the worker from work. The middle class has less motivation to work, because it is likely that his stuff will be stolen in this crime ridden society. And so getting rid of rent is one way to take a bite out of crime, by allowing the workers to own and retain the profits of their labor.

Corps vs. Co-ops

Another way that the rich steal from the poor is corporations. Corporations are the foundation of Wall Street. And Laissez-Faire promoters will tell you that corporations are the source of most jobs. Actually corporations were invented relatively recently in history. So they are not necessary for an economy. They help us do large projects that require the pooling of capital. But there is an alternative, which is Co-ops.

Corporations allow the rich once again to steal from the poor. The stockholders are people with money. They choose corporations that pay the most on the Bottom Line. Thus they vote with their pocketbook for corporations, which have the least costs, which thus cut wages as much as possible. And because jobs are so scarce, and because corporations control most jobs, they can use that leverage to cut the wages a lot. Thus the rich owners are stealing from the poor workers by taking a slice off their wages before they are paid.

And why are jobs scarce? Because the rich owners cut jobs periodically on purpose. The periods of economic growth make them money from the profits that belong to the workers. And the periods of economic recession make them money because it allows them to lay off higher paid workers, and then rehire experienced workers at less pay, thus lowering their costs. If that causes a few people to be homeless or hungry, who cares? Because the Bottom Line is always going up for the rich who are stealing from the poor. But again this type of greed is killing that 'goose.' Eventually there will be no one left to profit from.

In a corporation, the owners are the stockholders, who in large part have nothing to do with the operation of the company. They simply invest their savings in the mutual fund that pays the best. Their only concern is the Bottom Line. And because they are the owners, the only real concern of the company then is the Bottom Line. If they can get away with it, they will cut costs to increase that Bottom Line no matter who it hurts. Their only real concern with wages, or working conditions, or pollution, is to cut costs. We saw this at its worst in the Sweatshops two centuries ago. So to protect us from this type of greed, we made laws that hack at the symptoms, but do nothing against the root of the problem.

We made a minimum wage. But is that what workers really want and need? Can anyone really survive on minimum wage? We cut down the hours to 40 per week. And this simply resulted in people having two full-time jobs to survive. We have an EPA, which is infiltrated by Big Business bribes, and thus does little against pollution. We have OSHA, which is supposed to make the workplace safer, but mostly makes a lot of money for lawyers, and still most workers are miserable at their jobs. Fixing the symptoms does not work. The root of the problem lies in the institution of the Corporation.

"Corporation: An ingenious device for obtaining profit without individual responsibility." Ambrose Bierce

The purpose of incorporating is to remove responsibility from the individual owners for the actions of the corporation. In this way if a corporation is sued, the personal assets of the owners cannot be taken. Thus the purpose of corporations is to allow people to do things that are illegal or immoral without risking personal harm if they are caught. So if my company pollutes because of the decision of the board to cut costs, the individuals cannot be tried as criminals. And because the corporation is not a real person, if it goes to jail, who cares? If the government is supposed to protect us from theft and other crimes, then it should protect us from corporations, which are by definition criminal organizations.

The alternative is co-ops. In a co-op the workers own the business. They are also concerned with the Bottom Line because that is the source of their income. But they have other concerns also. They want good wages for the workers, since the shareholders are the workers. They will thus not pay themselves minimum wage, but a percentage of the profits. This of course motivates them to produce more, not just show up to punch their time card.

But they also want good work conditions, and they are willing to spare a little of their wage to accomplish that. After all, if we have to spend so much of our lives at work, does it have to be miserable, if we have the power to do something about it?

And what about pollution? If we live near the factory, as workers do, we do not want it polluting our community. We are motivated selfishly to stop the pollution, not just to comply with EPA standards. And we certainly will not try to get around EPA regulations, because our purpose includes not polluting our neighborhood, not just the Bottom Line.

If all corporations were converted to co-ops, we would have no need for an inept EPA and all the other regulatory agencies that are good at sucking up tax dollars and not much else. By marrying the purpose of the workers with ecology, we would boost ecology like never before. Ecology would not be opposed by business, but supported by business. Instead of having to fight politically against big business for every inch of ecology, we could have the genius and resources of the market place working for it. We could go green over night and at the same time get rid of those expensive government agencies that have failed to do the job.

Now if you combine the co-op issue with the rent issue, we find a major reason that small businesses have so much difficulty. Rent on commercial property is out of sight. A small shop often pays $4000 a month in rent alone. This means that it has to make a huge amount of money that it pays to some rich guy, before its workers see any of their profits. Big conglomerates can weather a recession, but the little guys lose their shirts.

The only way to change this is for the co-op workers to outright own the land that they work. So when mortgages are dissolved for primary homes, the same thing has to happen for co-ops that rent commercial space. The owners of that space then would have to hand it over to the co-ops that operated there, or set up his own shop there. Otherwise some rich guy is stealing a huge hunk of the profits of the workers once again. Currently you will see lots of empty retail spaces. This is because the little guys went bankrupt. If they did not have to pay that excessive rent, they could work and make less profit and keep the economy going.

Copyrights and Patents

Copyrights and Patents are another piece of propaganda that is used to steal from the poor. The hype goes that they are designed to promote invention by giving the inventor the rights to his invention. However what normally happens is that the inventor, without the means of mass producing or selling his creation, will sell his rights to a large company. That company will make the items or sell the books at great profit to the rich owners. The inventor or writer can and often gets only 2% of the profits. The guys who do the work making the thing or selling it in the stores will get minimum wage. And so a law which is supported, because it is supposed to help the little guy, is actually another means for the wealthy to make money from their money.

In the Bible there are no Copyright or Patent laws. It is the producers and sellers who do the work that make the full profit. If a person invents something, so he can produce more, then he makes a higher wage. Or if a person invents something and sells his idea to many people that do this work, he can make more money than the measly 2% he would have made under the Patent law that is supposed to protect his profits. On the other hand, he is just as motivated to invent without the patent law, because it will help him produce more and thus increase the profits from his work.

Under co-ops, research and invention can be funded in the same way and to the same level as corporations do. But the increase in production will be seen in the increase of profits, which will go directly to the workers. And it should since the workers provided part of their profits to fund the research activity of the co-op.

The Bottom Line

If these reforms were implemented, what would be the difference in the wages for the average worker? I ask this because when you start adding it up, it is much, much larger than one might expect.

Let's use some round numbers so that you can easily understand the concept. Each person's case will be different in numbers obviously. But if you understand this concept, you can plug your numbers in and see how it will work out for you.

Rent or payments on a home loan account for the majority of a person's wage. Let's say 50%. So if you make $4000 a month, you are paying a rich landlord $2000, leaving you $2000 of spendable income.

But if you worked at a co-op instead of a corporation, you would probably be making twice as much or more. So your wage would be $8000 a month instead. This means that the rich have stolen $6000 from you already.

But what are you going to do with that $2000 of spendable cash. You are going to spend it on your car, food, clothes, medical, education, etc. so that you can go to work. But why are those products so expensive? It is because some rich guy gets a cut. If you paid only the wages of the workers, you would pay half as much. For example if you pay $400 a month for your car, $200 of that probably goes to the workers that contributed to the manufacturing, transporting and mining involved. The other $200 goes to the owners of the companies involved.

How do I know this? If you take your car to be repaired, you might have to pay $60 an hour, but the mechanic is only getting $20 of that. Another $10 may be spent on equipment and the guy that cleans up and the secretary at the front desk. So that leaves half, or $30 for the owner of the shop. This means that of that $2000 that you spend on necessities, a group of rich guys are stealing $1000 of that. This means that you are actually only paying $1000 for the wages of the workers that produce items or services that you use.

But if the workers who produce those items for you worked at a co-op also, they would be getting twice the pay also. This means that you would still be paying $2000 for these things, but that entire amount would actually go to worker, rather than half of it being stolen.

Now if you subtract that $2000 from your real profit of $8000, you see that you have $6000 left over every month for saving for a rainy day. While you cannot make interest on that amount, the amount itself is much more than if you saved $10 or even $100 after most of your income was stolen, and then got interest. If you add that up over a life time of work, you could retire at age 60 with enough to live on for a long time. With 40 years of work times 12 months times $6000, you would have nearly 3 million dollars saved. If you figure that you only have to spend $2000 a month to live on, you could live on your retirement fund for 120 years.

This is nothing compared to the income of billionaires, but who needs to be a billionaire, if your money is not your security. You can only spend so much on toys. And if money is not your security, then you will feel free to give to the needs of others from your abundance, rather than horde it. That would give you a sense of fulfillment from contributing to your community by work, which is much more important than piles of money.

As you can see, we could all be working in a pleasurable job and making plenty of money to live comfortably, if we just made laws protecting the workers from the theft by the rich, so that they could keep their full profits from their work. This is fully protecting the profits from work, motivating work, while outlawing profits made from the possession of money, de-motivating theft.

Culture of Lawsuits

Why is it that if a person loses his job that he does not simply start his own business? With a few thousand dollars a guy should be able to set up a hotdog stand, or some other small one-man business. Aside from the prohibitively high rent on commercial properties, the fact is that most people are afraid of starting a business, because they would then be subject to being sued for something that is totally out of their control.

One of the justifications for the high cost of healthcare is the threat of lawsuits. While the big corporations can afford the best lawyers to stave off this problem, it is prohibitive to the little guy. Thus this culture of lawsuits is actually advantageous to the conglomerates, because it reduces their competition.

I used to work at a check cashing place. We had to keep a card on each customer that included information on each check that they cashed. Our concern was that the check would not bounce. But I noticed that the income of one customer was quite strange. He came in every week or so with a check for a large round amount: $3000, $4000, $5000, etc; a huge amount back in those days. And each check was from a different company. Each was some retail store. Now if he was doing some service, the amounts would not be round numbers, and he would have repeat customers. But instead there was not a single repeat customer. So I figured that this person was going around town slipping on a grape and suing these companies, who were then settling out of court. If they took it to court, it would have cost them more in court and lawyer fees, even if they won, not to mention the risk of losing.

Now the Bible has laws about safety. It is our obligation as company owners to put a rail around places that a person might fall off of for example. (Deuteronomy 22:8) This applies to making things as safe as possible. If a grape falls on the floor it needs to be cleaned up in a timely manner. But if someone is throwing a grape down and then slipping on it, how can you do anything about that? The buyer has some responsibility to watch where he is going.

Our Constitution and the Bible require that a person is innocent until proven guilty. It is therefore required that a business be proven negligent before it can be punished. The problem is that we have two different forms of jurisprudence in our country, with two different requirements of evidence. In criminal cases, the shadow of a doubt level of evidence is required. But in civil cases, the judge must decide for the person he thinks is more believable, without a need for real evidence. For example a person can be acquitted of murder in the criminal case due to lack of evidence, and then be sued by the family of the victim and take all his money without evidence.

But in the Bible there is no separation between civil and criminal cases. Instead any compensation for the victim is given as part of the judgment in the criminal case. So in the case of a murder trial if the person is acquitted, he cannot be later sued in civil court for the same offense.

This simple change in our law would eliminate the frivolous cases completely. If a person has not committed a crime, he should not be forced by the courts to compensate someone for damages. If there has been legitimate damages, then a victim can bring that to the attention of the Criminal Court. In Criminal Court the accused would be afforded all the rights given to those who are accused of crime. Why is it that those who are not accused of crime can be punished in Civil Court without the rights routinely given to a criminal?

Why is it that we feel a need for civil lawsuits? It is because our criminal cases do not adequately punish the criminals. The purpose of punishing criminals is to deter crime.

There are many stats out there that are used to show that punishment does not deter crime. But those stats compare two areas that are both woefully lacking in punishment. These stats are often quoted against capital punishment for example. They compare states that have capital punishment with those that do not. The difference in the amount of murders are negligible.

But think about how many murderers are actually given capital punishment in those states where it is allowed. Less than one percent of the murderers are actually executed. And if you compare that to the amount of murderers that not caught or convicted that percentage goes down much farther. The likelihood that that you will get executed for a murder in one of those states is negligible. So of course there is no deterrent factor. But if you compared the amount of murders in that state to a country that executed all murderers, you would see a huge difference in the amount of violent crime.

So to fix our legal system, we need to make a number of changes. First we need to get rid of Civil Courts and compensate victims in Criminal Court. Second we need to up the punishment significantly. If you figure that many criminals get away with most of their crimes due to lack of evidence, the punishment should not be for the single crime, but as a deterrent based on all the crimes that were not solved. This means that all first degree murderers should be executed, period. It means that thieves should pay five times what they stole, instead of just the amount they were convicted for. We are so lackadaisical about our punishment that we are sending the message that it is a normal and acceptable thing to be a criminal in this country. And if it is legal for the rich to steal from the poor by interest and rent, then crime of all kinds is ok.

We need to protect the accused citizen copiously, because he may be innocent. But once the evidence has proven that he is guilty beyond the shadow of a doubt, we need to let the hammer fall.

The fact that we are supposed to be innocent until proven guilty brings up a number of other practices in our country that are unconstitutional. This requires what is called 'due process of law.' This means that a crime must be committed and a decision must be made by a court before a punishment can be given. This may sound simple enough, but the ramifications of this distinction are far reaching.

From this we know that we should not torture people to get a confession. Obviously that is punishing someone before they are convicted. Nor can the government punish someone for no reason, without a crime having been committed at all. We expect these kinds of abuses from an autocratic society like Nazi Germany. What makes them autocratic is that their system of law is that people are guilty until proven innocent. This gives carte blanch power to the government.

So this means there can be no blanket laws to punish people without a conviction. A blanket law is not due process of law, but rather changes our system to guilty until proven innocent. The purpose of that clause in the Constitution is to specify the type of legal system that we are under.

An example of this issue against blanket laws is that a search cannot be done prior to a court making a decision about a crime that has already been committed. This means that it is unconstitutional to do random searches such as the ones done routinely at airports now, or routine wiretaps on citizens like the NSA does. If we want to do random searches for protection in a new type of situation, the Constitution requires a Constitutional Amendment to do so. It requires us to change our fundamental system of law, to guilty until proven innocent. But instead this was done by the stroke of a pen by one man, when he signed that executive order. By definition that makes him a dictator. And the few that spoke up about it were largely ignored because we operate on fear rather than principle. On the other hand, we can do any kind of search we want on foreigners traveling in our country, since our Constitution only applies to the citizens of our country.

This also applies to many of our regulations. If they require inspections prior to a court decision about a crime, then they are not allowed. Instead the Bible requires that safety measures be done by the citizens, but not inspected by the government. If a violation is reported by a citizen and there is evidence of a crime, then a deterrent punishment should be imposed to deter such a violation, meaning that an inspection can then be done to gather evidence about the crime. But general inspections assume that the general population is guilty until proven innocent by passing the inspection.

This also applies to licenses. All things are legal to the citizen until a Constitutional Amendment is made to take it away. The clause about 'life, liberty and the pursuit of happiness,' in the Declaration of Independence, guarantees this. If we assume that the general population is guilty until proven innocent, then we can test people before giving a driving license or any other kind of license. But if we believe that citizens are innocent until proven guilty, then we should only punish people who cause crashes. Again it should be a punishment that is severe enough to deter people from causing crashes. Traffic laws and class requirements can be made to ease the flow of traffic and determine who caused the crash, but should not have punishments for violating them unless the violation causes a crash.

And while we are talking about traffic fines, this system is set up to favor the rich once again. If a speeding fine is a flat $600, that is prohibitive to the poor, but it is pocket change to the rich. Thus the rich are allowed to speed, while the poor are not. To be equitable, fines should be based on the income of the violator, in order to deter everyone from crime. On the other hand, if it was illegal for the rich to steal the wages away from the workers, and everyone had to work equally for his wages, this huge income disparity would not exist, and this issue would be mute.

Precedent Law verses Legislative Law

Another thing that is broke in our legal system in Precedent Law. There are two kinds of law systems in history, Legislative Law and Precedent Law. Legislative Law is where the legislature alone can make laws and the courts merely interpret the laws. In Precedent Law, the judges add to the legislated law by their judgments. They legislate from the bench. And later cases site these Precedent Laws as law that other judges must abide by as much as Legislated Law.

Now if you learned anything in school about our Constitution, you learned that we separate the three branches of government, the Legislative, the Executive and the Judicial. Only the legislature is allowed to make laws. It is unconstitutional for the judges or the President to make laws. And yet if you go to law school, most of your studies will be on Precedent Laws made by judges. And when you go to court, it will be these laws made by judges that will have the most bearing on the case. If a law or even the Constitution is contradicted by a law made by a judge, then the judge's law stands.

The separation of the powers of the branches has been abrogated and the Judicial Branch now has supreme authority. Innocent people are afraid of going to court because they have no idea of the outcome. Not only are the laws too complicated to understand in the first place, they can also be changed by the judge during the trial.

For example, going back to that murder case where the murderer is acquitted and then later sued in civil court and loses. All of that is going on because of laws made by judges, not laws made by the legislature. If you remember the O.J. Simpson case this may be familiar to you. One of the main reasons that murderers get off is because some vital piece of evidence is not allowed in court. Most people think this is because of the Constitution, which does not allow illegal searches or seizures. But what is actually happening is that a judge ruled that if evidence is gathered illegally, then it cannot be used against the accused. But that is not what the Constitution says. It only says that it is illegal to gather evidence that way. If a search is illegal then the policeman that did it committed a crime and should go to trial and be convicted. But it has no bearing on the case of the murderer. How can a jury make the best decision, if the judge is deliberately withholding evidence from them? And why is he doing that? It is because of a law made by a judge that is by definition unconstitutional.

If we simply outlawed the suppression of evidence, so that jurors could have access to all the evidence, then our trials would come to much better verdicts.

On the other hand, many people accused of crime are convicted without enough evidence to prove it. This is because jurors are tired of criminals getting away with murder, literally. They understand that our criminal procedures are broke, so they lash back by convicting people when there is still a shadow of doubt, because of lack of evidence. If they do not like the guy, they convict him because they are fed up with the system. Thus letting criminals off by suppression of evidence causes innocent people to later be convicted. Instead of protecting the rights of the accused it destroys the deterrent purpose of our judicial system, because convictions are not based on evidence, but on the luck of the draw.

If you think about it, who is more likely to be convicted, the criminal who planned his getaway, or the bystander that reported it to the police? We are sending the wrong message. Innocent people are more afraid of the courts and the police, while criminals are simply required to do their crimes well. Luckily for the criminals, we provide free education in doing crime well in the form of our prisons.

Did you know that in Bible Law there are no prisons? All crime is punished by either execution or fine. And a person who cannot pay the fine has the option of selling himself into indentured servitude for seven years. During that time, he would be required to live with a family where he can learn how to do a business and conduct his affairs honorably. And when his time is up, his master is required to give him the basic tools for that new business, so he has nothing stopping him from making a legitimate living. (Deuteronomy 15:13-14)

Compare that to putting him in with a bunch of hardened criminals that will teach him to use various methods of crime to survive. Those that are tougher than the others get what they want. The others lose everything and get raped. Are our prisons any better than a foreign prison where the guards rape the inmates, if the inmates are raping the inmates?

Prisons are a huge waste of tax dollars. We should get rid of them altogether. This means that we have to execute every one convicted of major violent crimes and instate indenturing to pay fines for minor crimes. In this way the criminals are paying for their crimes, not the tax payers.

This Brings Us to Taxation.

The Bible talks about a flat 10% tax. The purpose of the graduated tax system is to get some equity by evening the income disparity. But this simply is another means of stealing from the worker, which de-motivates the worker from working. If you know that you will have to pay more taxes if you make more money, then you are motivated to make less money by working less.

On the other hand because the graduated tax system is so complicated, a good tax lawyer can eliminate your taxes almost completely. So the rich who can afford these good tax lawyers pay little under that system. Thus the only people that actually benefit from a graduated tax are the superrich, who use propaganda to make poor workers think that they will benefit from this system. So the graduated tax system, which is designed to make the rich pay more, actually makes the workers pay more and motivates people to cheat the system legally or illegally, or to get on welfare. Or if you steal something and go to prison you can beat the tax system too. So a graduated tax system is causing more problems and not accomplishing its intention.

But a flat tax that is not too high motivates people to work harder and make more, because they get to keep the same percentage no matter how much they make. And instead of concentrating on loopholes and scams, they can concentrate on producing more of whatever they produce. With this encouragement to work, a small tax of 10% would bring in more revenue than the current graduated tax that has contributed to the fact that more than 50% of the people in this country do not work.

The main reason that deductions are part of the tax system is because they provide the IRS with clues about whether the person's income is about right, or if he should be audited. Because you get money for the information, you gladly give it to them, and incriminate yourself. Again this is presuming taxpayers to be guilty until proven innocent, and thus giving undue power to IRS agents. They can punish you without a trial and without the rights of an accused.

On the other hand if we become a law abiding society, we will no longer tend to cheat on our taxes. If our taxes are going to a Government that is guaranteeing our freedom and land, we will want it to have 10% of our pay so that it can do that. It is only when the government uses taxes for things that we voted against that we resent it. And that will go away with Exclusive Communities as we will discuss next.

Because we will not routinely audit citizens, we will have to rely on the deterrent of a harsh punishment to do the job. I think anyone convicted of cheating on his taxes under such a just system should lose his citizenship, since he is obviously not wanting to support the nation. And only if someone reports cheating, will an investigation happen, because citizens are presumed innocent till proven guilty. And the one being investigated will have a trial and all the rights of an accused criminal.

At the same time, this will allow us to cut the IRS to practically nothing, so that it is not another unnecessary tax-sucking agency that we have to pay for.

The purpose of the graduated tax then is better served by the other reforms that we have discussed to keep the rich from stealing from the workers in the first place. If everyone's income is based solely on the work he does, then the disparity of income will not be based on the advantage of wealth, but on the amount of work. If workers get more income from producing more, then there is no moral reason to take that profit from them with a graduated tax.

Exclusive Communities

We discussed before that we have to change our paradigm, so that our security no longer comes from our accumulated money, but from our community. You may have been wondering how that works out, because if your community is like most, it is hard to imagine depending on it for much, particularly our security. These people would walk by you while you were being murdered and never lift a finger. So giving up my wealth leveraging and expecting my neighbors to be my security instead is rather farfetched.

Well the only way this will work is with closed or exclusive communities. Our nation used to be made of Exclusive Communities. It was not until the integration issue became law in the fifties and sixties that this changed. Integration was designed to help blacks get out of the ghetto, so that they would have an opportunity to get wealth, just like the whites. But has it worked? Blacks still have much more poverty and much fewer jobs than the whites. So my conclusion is that it does not work. The reason for that is that again we are attacking one symptom rather than the root of the problem. The root of the problem is allowing the rich to steal from the poor. If the blacks did not have to pay rent and interest to the rich white guys, then they would not be disadvantaged. It is the theft of work profits that causes minorities to be de facto slaves of the establishment.

Prior to integration, we had a representative government, where each community and state was unique. Each state was originally based on a common denomination of Christianity, such as the Puritans of Massachusetts or the Catholics of Maryland. Thus if you wanted to live with like-minded people, you could. And if you were with like-minded people, you could depend on them to have your back. It was only when people that were not like-minded moved into your neighborhood that you became afraid of your neighbors and had to lock your doors.

Even if you are in a criminal gang, you can depend on your neighbors to have your back. If the gang is to hold together, the crime must be directed outside of your little circle. In fact I am proposing that each neighborhood become organized like a gang in some ways. Of course this would be a gang that is not criminal. Instead of getting its income from theft or drugs, these neighborhood gangs would be made of legitimate workers. It would be built around some sort of business, with its own basic shops and amusements within walking distance.

It would have its own local security plan based on the druthers of the like-minded people of that community. They could have a regular local police department. Or they could have armed citizens. It might have a defensible perimeter. Because they are like-minded people they could set up their laws in any way that they want. Anyone coming into the neighborhood uninvited would be trespassing and subject to prosecution under whatever laws the community saw fit to implement. As a result the community would become a family or team that works together for mutual benefit, rather than a group of differing people that may hate each others' guts.

Thus the community would insure security in the territory of the community, from outsiders. If an outsider comes into the community, he is scrutinized and held at a distance until he is cleared, based on whatever rules, or criterion, or profiling the community thought prudent. Under our current system a terrorist could live next door and you would never know it, until the bomb blew up your kids.

These communities would inevitably divide on lines of values or religion. And that is a good thing. A lot of the friction politically in this country comes from people whose purpose is very different than the voters next to him. One group may want Sunday as a Sabbath, while others may want Saturday, or Friday, or some may want their stores open seven days a week. If they are in their own communities, the fighting about these issues goes away and everyone gets what they want.

Under our current form of integrated democracy, no one gets what they want. Everyone has to compromise. The anti-abortionists have to put up with some level of murder of infants in their society. But the pro-abortionists are not allowed to do certain kinds of abortions as a compromise with the pro-life voters. And both groups have to spend huge amounts of money and effort campaigning against the other just to keep that compromise in place. All that money and effort every election year, and still neither side really gets what it wants, even if they win the election. But if we simply divided into separate communities, which made their own separate laws, we could all get exactly what we wanted and we could use that money and effort on something we could keep and enjoy.

Each community would be separate with its own separate laws, rather than have national or state laws that address lifestyle issues, based on middle of the road compromises. And each person could live in whatever community he wanted, so he could enjoy the exact laws that he wanted. If the community decided to change or add a law that you did not like, then you would have a choice of moving to a different community, or putting up with a minor issue to remain with your friends, depending on how important it was to you.

In a multi-cultural democracy, politicians learn to think small. Any proposed legislation has to be about one small issue, and it has to be near the middle of the road, or too many people will find something to disagree with. Think about illegal drugs. Some people want to legalize it and promote it, and others want to eradicate it with the death penalty. But because there is so much tug-of-war politically on the issue, we have wishy-washy laws on it. The voters who are against it, must vote for laws that are a little bit stricter, while those who are for it vote for laws that are a little bit looser. As a result of these middle of the road laws, we have more illegal drug use, and more drug arrests in the U.S. than any other nation. It makes a huge amount of people into criminals. Presidents admit to this crime, meaning that it is ok to be a successful and respectable citizen, and commit crime. People know that everything is illegal in this country and so being a criminal is normal. If we had the laws that we wanted, we could all go back to being law abiding and get to do anything that we wanted.

Separate communities would allow those who are against drugs to eradicate it from their community, by clamping down hard. And it would allow those who are for it to legalize it completely in their community. And if some people want to perpetually fight their neighbors about political issues, they can set up a community that does that. Everyone would get what they want. We would no longer have to think small in politics. They could enact any law that they wanted and not have to worry about someone down the street voting against it. Instead of your vote being cancelled out by people who differ with you, your vote could be used to create your own idea of utopia in your own neighborhood.

Think about the amount of money that goes into political campaigns. Why do we do that? If you want more social services, what are you going to get for your money and effort? After your vote is canceled by the right wingers, you will get very little.

But if you are in a community of like-minded people, that makes all your lifestyle laws, the Federal offices will become less important. You can get any law that you want, as long as the Federal Government guarantees your community's right to do whatever it wants. And every community is going to agree on that and vote for that kind of Federal candidate. Exclusive Communities will suddenly make us all agree with each other on this fundamental level, and allow us all to have complete freedom to have exactly what we want.

What Exactly is Freedom?

'Freedom' is an elusive term that is used to support anything from anarchy to dictatorship. Thus the term 'Freedom' is meaningless unless you define what you want freedom for.

We think of freedom as multi-cultural democracy, where everyone has the 'freedom of religion.' But if my practice of religion is restricted by the voter next door who wants to do things different, then how free am I really. If I can only practice my religion inside a private church and not anywhere else, and even that has certain restrictions, do I really have religious freedom? The right to 'believe' anything you want is enjoyed by inmates in concentration camps. Is that the freedom that you aspire to? If you want freedom to practice Muslim Law, then your idea of freedom is very different than the Christian next door, or the Atheist.

But Exclusive Communities allow every group to have the type of freedom that they want. The Atheist can teach evolution in his community, and the Creationist can teach creation in his community, and nobody has to put up with something they do not like from their neighbor. If you want to require burkas, or restrict their use, or make them optional, you can. Everyone gets exactly what they want and does not have to put up with laws against their practices. That is real Freedom to not only 'believe' what you want, but to act on those beliefs.

Exclusive Communities also require everyone to take responsibility for their own decisions. If one group has one idea about dealing with crime and the other group has another idea, they end up doing some compromise, because their votes cancel each other. Then when the middle of the road answer does not work, both groups blame the other for causing the problem.

But if they separated into their own communities, both could get the solution that they wanted. If one solution works, then great. If the other solution does not work, then they will be able to blame no one but themselves. They can learn from their mistakes and change. But when we do the compromise system, the wrong decision never really gets tried, and they continue to vote for it and never learn. Separate communities can get us out of that rut and foster success from experimenting.

Helping Our Extended Family

If I have a community of like-minded people, I do not mind helping those in need. But if I have to give my taxes to someone who is lazy, or who is voting against what I want, then I resent it. We are motivated to help the members of our household, when they are sick, or young, or old. We do this because we have a relationship with them. And we do not mind it, because they either helped us in the past, or will help us in the future. Our friends are a part of our security. Instead of gravitating toward taking charity from strangers, we would gravitate toward helping our friends by hard work.

By extending this circle of security out farther from our immediate family to our community of like-minded friends, we have more security. The bigger our gang, the more difficult it is for criminals to attack us. The bigger our gang is, the greater calamity we can forestall. In fact the only time the State or Federal Government would have to help us is in the case of an extremely widespread disaster. And we would be better organized, so that we would need less help in such a disaster. The rest of the time, the work of the community can take care of all our needs as individuals fluctuate.

I heard a revealing stat: The average newly-wed in America is $3000 in debt, while the average newly-wed in Japan has $20,000 in the bank. Japan uses an extended family approach to economy. Children stay in their parents' homes longer. They often get a job with the family business.

Extended families are similar to Exclusive Communities in many ways. The family wants the children to succeed and helps them get the skills to help the family business. In the same way Exclusive Communities naturally want to help each other succeed.

A Different Concept of Home

Currently your primary home is your primary investment. With the current tax laws, a primary home is the best investment you can make. It will appreciate in value because land will go up in price as the population grows. And the population will always be growing. Plus you can write off the interest on your taxes. Thus it is a typical investment scheme to buy as big of a house as your budget can afford, so that you get the most appreciation in value. It was because of this that people lost so many homes recently when the value of homes went down. You see this system is actually to the advantage of the banks. They either get more interest or more properties, regardless of the economy.

But another reason that we want a large yard is so that we can be as far as possible from our neighbors, because they are obnoxious. With Exclusive Communities all your neighbors will be like-minded and so you will not need to get far away from their obnoxious music or loud motorcycles, or their smoke that drifts into your window. Instead we will want to maximize our socializing time with our like-minded friends that live next door.

So instead of buying a big home that we really do not need, we will get a relatively small private apartment that is easy to clean, next to common areas, where we can visit with neighbors. We can have both full privacy when we want, and plenty of social opportunities. Plus it will be within walking distance of work and shops and entertainment. No daily commutes. Instead we can come home for a leisurely lunch.

If your home is a given, rather than an investment to leverage money away from a buyer/worker, then you will want a home that will fit your purposes exactly. It will no longer be important to live in a home that has more resale value by being appealing to someone else. And it does not have to be bigger so you can one day make more money. Mansions will become multi-family buildings. Apartments will designate more spaces as common areas and become just as pleasant as mansions.

And because it is yours, you will invest into fixing it up, rather than tearing it apart as many renters do, when they get mad at the landlord for stealing from their work profit. You will work together as tight teams of like-minded people to make your common areas really nice, because they belong to you.

Because we are not wasting money on homes that are hardly used, we can pool our money to make great common areas. That home gym with one limited machine that normally gathers dust, can be an elaborate community gym, where we can encourage each other to work out. Instead of that small kitchen, we can have a common gourmet kitchen and share the cooking. Or we can do away with the kitchen altogether, hire a professional chef, and have a community cafe where we can go for healthy common meals or get a snack any time. And because we are not sharing these common areas with strangers, who may vandalize them, we do not mind paying for their upkeep. We can set up our lifestyle in much more efficient and desirable ways that are not dictated by silly things like tax exemptions, or poverty, or city codes voted in by some idiot that you don't even like.

The cultural concept of domicile will change radically. Shared spaces will become more desirable and possible. Living alone and powerless in big houses in the suburbs will be a thing of the past, though that option will still be possible if you are a real loner. If we want to get off by ourselves, we can have that in our community too because we are in a community of like-minded people. If our community wants a big forest for camping, we can have that. We will be powerful teams of friends living together and having plenty to make our spaces exactly like we want them to be.

Is it really better to hang onto that big empty house that you have to spend so much time on cleaning and repairing? How much real time do you have to do things after you have finished the paperwork for the insurance company and done the commute?

Money is actually a pile of useless paper. It is not even good for a warming fire. Is it more important than a pleasurable space and friends? The things that we want are produced by work not money. Money without work produces nothing. But work without money can still produce anything. Do you want a car so you can do a daily commute to a miserable office? Do you want a Mutual Fund, so that you can have money to pay the HMO when you get old? Do you want to constantly fight with the voter next door on every little political issue, and end up with a compromise that neither of you want?

We are so used to getting very little of what we really want, and giving so much of our work profit to someone else. And yet we clutch onto those crumbs with white knuckles. I am talking about opening our eyes to the possibilities. We can have anything we can imagine. We just have to pour our work into it, and outlaw the stealing of other people's work profits.

The primary thing that we have to do to create Exclusive Communities is to legalize them.

It is revealing that when we talk about Exclusive Communities, we think of communities that are restricted to wealthy people. It is against the law to exclude people from your community on the basis of values or religion. But it is ok to make all the houses in your neighborhood so high priced that only the rich can live there. Do they have their own security? Of course. But for those of us,

who are not rich, it is illegal to have an Exclusive
Community that has its own security. Poor or middle-
class Exclusive Communities are called 'militias' or
'gangs' and are eradicated by SWAT teams.   This is the
rich operating in the background to disrupt their
opposition, so they can stay in power. Their opposition is
vulnerable, while they are secure behind their gates.
Legalizing Exclusive Communities for all people based on
whatever criterion each community chooses is ultimate
freedom.

Self-Sustaining and Non-Polluting

There is a major battle politically in the nation between the industrialists and the tree huggers. This concept of Exclusive Communities that are more autonomous would effectively end that war. It is the emphasis on the Bottom Line that makes ecology unimportant to corporations. But with co-ops, ecology is very important because its shareholders, the workers, live next to the company. The pollution of the company would affect the shareholders more than anyone else.

Big Corporations like to bribe the government for the right to pillage resources that are thousands of years in the making, without having to even buy the land. Then they pack up and pillage another area. And because the shareholders don't live there, they don't care what it looks like when they leave. Pillaging is just plain better for the Bottom Line.

The Co-op Community on the other hand will naturally want to use resources responsibly, in a more sustained way, in the area where its shareholders live. They will not want to destroy the natural beauty of their home, enabling them to continue to prosper there in the long run.

This also calls for a more self-sustaining community. Because it will naturally want to insulate itself from the bad decisions of other communities, it will have a desire to be more self-sustaining.

This means less transportation costs. As more of our necessities are grown or made locally, there are less middlemen and lest truck exhaust. We could develop walking communities, where we work, live, shop and play within walking distance most of the time. This would also have a nice side-effect of taking a bite out of obesity. This could virtually eliminate smog and our dependence on foreign oil. We would have to buy fewer cars, because we would be driving a lot less. We could even have a small community pool of vehicles, maintained by the community mechanic, to borrow instead, when we needed to go out of town or pick up something large. This simple change in our culture could solve a myriad of problems.

Today, the tree huggers complain, but nobody who wants to get or keep a job will stand up with them. Corporations naturally pit jobs against sustaining the Earth. Co-op Communities put jobs and the Earth on the same side. It would be in our selfish interest as a community, that contains the factories that we work in, to do all the things that ecologists advocate. Instead of companies fighting against ecology, they would use their human and material resources to make the environment better for its worker-shareholder-residents. And we would be able to do those things in a reasonable manner that would fit our situation exactly, rather than according to some law made in Washington, by people that were thinking about some other place.

Instead of being one of the greatest polluters in the world, our country would lead in ecology by example. And we as national voters would be united against foreign polluters. Today foreign polluters are often a subsidiary of a U.S. Corporation. And because voters vote against ecology in favor of the economy, the U.S. does little against foreign polluters. But if we as Co-op Communities were united for ecology, we would use our leverage against foreign polluters who affect the Earth that we live in.

Community Health Care

Another area of greed is the health industry. Driven by the huge profits of the pharmaceutical companies, cartels have been instituted under the coordination of HMO's. While this results in some scientific breakthroughs, most of the drugs out today have only been tested in the short-term as required by the FDA. Later, as people start discovering the long-term effects of them, because they are dying, the lawyers make money off the system. But because of the immense money and thus power of the Health Cartels, the system keeps on spewing out these dangerous drugs.

Lyme disease is an example of how this power system created the problem and destroys those who are trying to bring these offenses to light. There are a couple of eye-opening documentaries out on this problem. (underourskin.com) Lyme disease was started as a biological warfare experiment using a syphilis like spirochete on ticks. It was done on an island off the East Coast, but birds spread the ticks to the mainland and it is now spreading exponentially. And yet the HMO's deny the very existence of chronic Lyme disease and will not pay for its treatment. Yet an experiment has found that 70% of Alzheimer's, ALS and Parkinson's patients tested positive for Lyme antibodies. This means that most of these people have been misdiagnosed and are dying because of a cover-up within the Health Cartels. And the panel that provides the official position on this disease is primarily made up of people that work for these pharmaceutical companies that pay them to keep their proprietary research secret. This means that getting accurate health information that does not promote the most profitable drugs is near to impossible.

Obama-care simply forces people to funnel their money into these cartels. It does nothing substantial about the price of health care, because it leaves the HMO's in charge of the Health Cartels. On the other hand, the Laissez-Faire system allows these cartels to leverage their money to steal from the poor legally, by monopoly tactics. Neither side is good for us. And both answers are leading us into an uncontrolled spiral of increasing health premiums.

Think about where the premium money goes. Very little of it goes to workers who make the drugs or do the medical procedures. The portion that goes to the insurance company goes mostly to the owners, not the salesmen. The portion that goes to the pharmaceutical companies goes mostly to the owners, not the production workers. The patent owners are the companies, while the actual inventors only get a small percentage of the profits, as we discussed above. It is our patent laws that allow the rich owners of these companies to steal from the patients and workers, by inflated prices. The portion that goes to the hospitals, goes mostly to the owners of the hospitals, not the doctors, nurses and medical assistants that work there.

In this most profitable of American industries, I find it shocking that many of the workers volunteer their services for free, in the hopes of getting a near minimum wage job sometime in the future. That sounds like slavery to me.

Exclusive Communities would break up the power of these Cartels. Since our insurance would be handled by the communities independently, the big insurance companies would no longer be needed. It is these big insurance companies that manage the Health Cartels in a way that they can take a huge cut off the top of insurance premiums. That cut would be eliminated by Exclusive Communities handling their own insurance for mutual benefit.

And by the elimination of those insurance companies, the cartels would fall apart. The doctors would work within a community for mutual benefit, not profit at the expense of patients. The pharmaceutical companies would no longer answer to the FDA, which they can bribe, but to these organized communities that expect long-term tests and results. Research and development, funded by co-ops, could spend just as much money on discoveries. But their primary goal would not be making a buck in the short term at any cost. Instead their primary goal would be really helping the patient, since their shareholders would be the patients.

Additionally, exercise, diet and happiness are more important in health than drugs. 30% of the people in this country are obese, which is causing a huge amount of unnecessary sickness, including certain types of diabetes, cancer and heart failure. Exclusive Communities will encourage good health practices, because they want the best for their friends, and because lowering actual sickness in the community means less work disruption and less money shelled out for cures. A doctor who never socializes with his patients cannot encourage them to exercise and eat right. But friends in a walking community can do that easily.

Thus Exclusive Communities would naturally lower the price of health care, while increasing its effectiveness. And because the community shares with its community members, healthcare would suddenly be provided to all. The prices would be based on the work of those that actually do the work, rather than having to give a cut to the rich owners of the companies, who do not do the work.

Community Education

Another type of Corporation that is killing us is education. We understand that education is essential for producing skilled workers. And so for the sake of the economy it should be expanded. However, the politicians just want to throw money at it by providing scholarships from tax dollars.

But even though they have the highest education, why are teachers the lowest paid workers, and yet at the same time the cost of education is skyrocketing? The main reason is that the owners of the schools are taking bigger cuts. If the teachers owned the schools as co-ops, the cost of education would be cut in half and the real wages of teachers would be doubled.

But what kind of an education does the average worker really need? He needs to learn how to do a job at the community factory. Who can train him to do that? His neighbors who work there. And they will be motivated to train him to do that job well, because he is their security. If that new guy takes his place on the assembly line and is making a good wage, then he will better be able to help that neighbor when that neighbor is sick or injured. Instead of competing for jobs, we will be motivated to get everyone in the community working and producing. And that means providing education necessary to do that job. And if that person has a good paying job, he can save up for higher education if he wants it. And since colleges are now co-ops, he can get that education for half the price.

In Free Enterprise, the market regulates its own prices by supply and demand. That is still true in this sharing economy. In fact it is more true because the rich cannot manipulate the market, but on the other hand it is not as harsh because of community support. If it is illegal to leverage their money to make more money, they can never get rich enough to take over like that. That means that prices will truly be regulated by simple supply and demand, not monopolies and power brokers. And this works for education too.

In Free Enterprise the rich eventually take over with monopolies and cartels and start artificially inflating the prices to their own advantage. In education, if there is high competition for jobs, then the price of education will go up, meaning that the cut of the owners of the schools goes up.

Schools teach subjects that were in demand years ago, when the teacher decided his major. But in the sharing economy, more teachers are part-time neighbors, who can make money producing things. If the things he is producing go down in price due to oversupply, then he will naturally want to spend more hours working to makeup his income. Also less people will want to be trained in a job that already has too many workers. He will not want to train others to do that job and glut the supply even more. But those in high demand jobs will want to train people, so that they can cut their hours down. And because their job is in high demand, it is paying more, and so they can afford to take time out for training. And it is to the advantage of community members to facilitate this training in various ways to get everyone producing, meaning that much of this training will be free.

Education will not be based on certificates as much. In the workplace a diploma is not as important as experience and the real ability and responsibility to do the job well. The community will be concerned that the person knows how to do his job and that he is doing something that is productive. They will know his ability to do that job by working beside him, which is much more accurate than a certificate. Thus the quality of his education will be regulated by his fellow workers who know each other. Certificates will become less important. The Federal and State Governments will lose control of education. Reputation in schools will take a more dominate role.

Also extraneous subjects required by the State will fall by the wayside in favor of practical subjects that will get the person up and running on the job quicker. The teachers will not be paid for the amount of hours that they teach, but for producing a trained worker. Thus they will get paid more for teaching quicker, not longer. The concept of a 'four year' degree will be less important, than a short course that will make someone into a good assistant, who can subsequently learn on job and with evening courses.

But education is not just for getting a higher paying job. Extraneous subjects are put into the curriculum to spark interest in culture. But a lot of kids do not think that American Lit is relevant, because they are concerned with getting knifed on the way home from school. They do not think these subjects will help them with real life concerns. They just take those classes to get a diploma and then flush the information.

But in a safe Co-op Community, young people will start work early as apprentices and start learning the value of contributing. Later, they will want to participate in other ways with the community, such as political or philosophic discussion. As a community we will want to explore and reach higher and go there together. Part or all of the community could pack up and go on an educational vacation together if they wanted. We will have leisure and resources to learn about other topics just to expand our minds. Those classes will then contain students that are more interested in the subjects, than shooting spit wads.

And because the community training is sponsored by like-minded people, courses can be tailored to the values and beliefs of that community. If they want to emphasize science or religion, they will have the freedom to do so. They can pray in class in their community and no one will complain. Or they can outlaw prayer in class and no one will complain, because all the people in that class are like-minded.

Community Networks

Each community will be relatively small and relatively self-sustaining. This means that it cannot possibly provide all the specialists required for every need. On the one hand people will need to live more simply. But the poor are already used to that, so that will be no big change for the majority. In fact the majority will have more than they currently experience under poverty.

But that does not mean that specialization is impossible. Each community will have its own specialty; its 'cash crop,' as it used to be called. That can be an actual crop, or it can be any other specialization that it exports for cash. A community could specialize in cancer care for example and take patients from other communities.

We have been talking about how face to face relations regulate the quality of care. And so if we go to another community for cancer care, how does that fit this concept? Where does the quality control come from in inter-community trade?

Each community will have to maintain a list of communities that provides evaluations. Customer evaluations are playing a greater role in the market place now thanks to the internet. But that list is only as reliable as the company that maintains that list. That is why each community will have to maintain its own list. As its members use other communities' products, the list will reflect the quality of those communities.

Another way to evaluate other communities is like-mindedness. If another community shares your values or religion, then that would indicate that it is more trustworthy. Today, when you go for healthcare or any other product, you have little idea if the person providing that service or product simply wants to make money, or if his agenda is more sinister. But you can be well assured that a like-minded community is not an enemy that wants bad things for you.

Thus by evaluations and like-mindedness, a network of trusted communities will develop. Within that network more specialization can be provided, than a single community can provide. As that network widens, so will the specialization increase. Additionally some trade can go on outside of that network of like-minded communities, based solely on quality. It will not be as trusted, but can fill in some specialization gaps when needed. This means that this community system can, through a network of communities, provide care and products that are just as specialized as our current market and more reliable than our current market. Self-sustainment means less transportation and pollution and cost, while networks of communities fills in the gaps as needed.

Advertising is another way that the wealthy leverage their money to make more money. The price of advertising goes up with better locations and agencies that are better at harnessing misinformation to gain market shares. Thus those who can afford the most expensive advertising are going to increase their profits at the expense of the little guys.

But without Copyrights and Patents and corporations, franchises that funnel part of the pay of local workers into the pockets of the rich will no longer exist. And thus the need for advertising will subside.

Instead a National Register, that provides information on each community's basic values and products, will provide basic searchable information on products made by the communities. Then the client driven community lists will organize that information for the customers. In this way each worker, no matter how small his company, will compete on the basis of true information, which is most important to the customer, such as common values and quality.

On the local level, there could be little clumps of like-minded communities that ban together to form a little town. Or if more participated, it could be a city. Each community would provide its piece of the economy, farming, resources, clothing, construction, etc. This would make the town very self-sustaining. They could situate the communities in such a way to efficiently facilitate production chains. The cotton farm could be next to the fabric plant, which is next to the clothing factory, which is next to the shops. Today we break up these activities into municipal zones to keep them far away from the residents, because of the pollution, thus legislating commutes. But that would not be a limiting factor with ecologically friendly Co-op Communities.

The defense perimeter could be around the town and they could pool their security resources for a more robust defense. And they would not mind spending time in these other communities, or be afraid of letting townspeople into their community, because they are all in the same value group.

Each community could have a first aid station, but one might have a doctor, another a nurse, and others just medics. These could treat most minor complaints. But if a more involved procedure was needed, they could meet at the doctor's clinic to perform it. Only more specialized needs would be referred to a nearby hospital, or specialist's clinic.

Each community could have a community café with a general menu and a specialty menu. If you wanted a sandwich, you could walk next door. But if you wanted Mexican that night, you could go to a nearby community. By pooling the resources of a number of like-minded communities, you could have a great deal of specialization and security in a local setting, and at the same time provide basics for each community.

In our current system those in the know use information from secret networks to get ahead. They use it to make better decisions in the stock market. And they try to keep that information away from the general public so that they can leverage it for greater profits.

The community system makes that network information more transparent. It allows everyone in the community to profit from it. The fact that this information is public means that substandard communities will be pressured to increase their quality. Thus network information is not used to promote yourself by pushing others down, but to build up everyone for general prosperity.

Technology

Specialization brings up the topic of Technology. Self-Sustaining communities may at first glance seem anti-technology. But as we just saw, specialization is just as prevalent in networks of communities. This means that technology could continue to advance at the same exponential rate as it is going today.

Prophets of our age are predicting that technology will continue to advance exponentially. Nanobots and Genetics are supposed to extend our life. Some predict that robots or cyborgs will take over the world in 40 years. Computing power is doubling every year.

But these prophets tend to focus on just the technology side of this issue. The moral side of the issue seems to be often ignored. What this exponential advance means to me is that in the future we can blow ourselves up much easier than we could before. If we do not learn to regulate technology by our morality, this is exactly what our future holds.

The escalating conflict embodied by 'Occupy Wall Street,' points out that before computers will be able to save us, we will destroy ourselves. If we inadvertently program our robots with the same blind greed that we currently rule with, they will be hostile to us. Thus changing our culture is more important than it has ever been, in the face of these powerful technologies.

New States

A more ambitious plan for communities could be to split up the country into new States divided by common values or religions. This could be done by everyone voting on the value or religion that they want. This would result in a list of values, each with a certain number of people. These values could include such things as religious beliefs, type of government, types of freedoms, basic laws, positions on various political issues, types of acceptable amusements, educational issues, etc. Essentially everyone would join one of hundreds of political parties; one that has your own exact values. Thus there would be as many parties as there are varied values and religions, some large and others small.

Each value group will get a portion of the country, based on a certain amount of land per persons in that party. Small groups may want to band together into a coalition of similar ideas to form a state. In this way every group gets a region of the country, which will become a new State.

You could start with the smallest group and let them choose where they want to be. By starting at the smallest groups, every group will have some resources. Otherwise some small groups may end up in a place with no water that is unviable. But a large group would have a large leftover territory that would have some resources somewhere. This means that the large groups would not have an undue advantage over the small groups.

Each new State would have like-minded voters and thus like-minded representatives that would truly represent them in Congress, instead of being just middle of the road types. This would make our representative type of government work once again. If all States have a similar mix of people, like they do today, the State form of representation and the Electoral College no longer make sense. A two party, middle of the road democracy emerges, which leaves all non-middle of the road people unrepresented. But if each State consists of different values, then its representatives will present in congress all the values of all the citizens.

Further this would allow networks of similar value communities to be located near each other, so that trade within that network requires less transportation. The new State could be more responsive to the people with regard to security and other laws. They could enact state laws if they wanted that would reflect the real will of the like-minded people in that State. Then within that state would be communities with various cash crops and specializations to provide all of their needs within a regional area. You could require State laws to be enacted only by three quarts vote, in order to provide each community in that State with maximum freedom for their own laws. Without this plan, a like-minded specialty hospital for example might be located on the other side of the country, instead of being within a few hundred miles of you.

This will take a more aggressive approach to moving people to their communities. But the value of having like-minded people together to support each other easier in the long run, I believe would justify this extra work.

After the new States were mapped out, the people could actually move at a leisurely pace. In the mean time the communities could start thinking and acting like communities. They could even start helping each other to some degree, even though their members are still spread out all over the country. They could hold elections and start organizing. They could pool some of their resources to accomplish the moving and setting up of their new home.

The Right to Secede

The Right to Secession is the cornerstone of freedom upon which our Constitution is built. It is the primary message of the Declaration of Independence. Without the Declaration of Independence, we would not have seceded from Britain, and we would still be under English Law, and the Constitution would not be worth the paper it is written on. The right to form your own government, when the one you are under is oppressing you, by making you do something you do not want to do, is the most fundamental freedom.

In this Exclusive Community model the most important thing is that each citizen is allowed to be in the type of community of his choice that has the right to make its own laws. Only in this way do people have the means of truly governing themselves in exactly the way that they want to be governed. This most fundamental freedom is the only way to insure that no one is oppressed by the government or the majority. Majority rule that makes minorities do things that they do not want to do is oppression, just as much as it would be if a dictator did that same thing to them.

Neither should States or networks be allowed to abridge that right. This freedom of individuals to reside in the community of their choice means that the Federal Government should use its power to guarantee that.

There should to be a Federal Free Zone where anyone can go to, if they want to leave their community for any reason. They can apply to join a different community, but that is subject to the approval of that community. If they are being oppressed and need to get out quickly, a Federal Free Zone would be a place to stay temporarily till things can get straightened out.

Also the Federal Government should investigate allegations of any community not letting people out who want to get out. Such a crime would be kidnapping and treason. Such a community, if convicted on undeniable evidence, should be disbanded and its perpetrators lose their citizenship. This one freedom, to not be oppressed by any community, or majority, or minority, is the most fundamental freedom that our Federal Government can enforce.

How does this affect criminal justice? If a person has the right to leave, does that mean a person convicted of a capital crime can just leave the community to avoid punishment? This case would be handled as an appeal. The convicted criminal would appeal his case to the State and then to the Federal level. If the law in that community is different than Federal law, he might be acquitted. But then he would have a record that would be considered when he applied to join some other community.

Or what about a thief, who cannot pay his fine, becomes an indentured servant? Someone pays his fine for the promise of working for him for seven years. And then the criminal decides to run away. Again this is his right to secede.

"You shall not deliver unto his master the servant which is escaped from his master unto you." Deuteronomy 23:15

But remember that the purpose of indenturing is to restore the thief to being a respected member of the community. If he does not fulfill his obligation, his citizenship is revoked and all the benefits of the community are removed, including the home he was living in. Thus serving the sentence is his voluntary means of being restored to the favor of his community.

On the other hand, if a person disagreed with a law, it would be prudent to leave the community before violating it. This is the right to secession that needs to be acknowledged by the community and the Federal Government. Each person should also have the right to leave the nation, if they have not already violated a law. In fact it might be good to grant banishment as an option instead of execution. But that would be dependent on some other country's desire to take them in.

One example of that is the planning of a Terrorist activity that was never carried out. In this case the person did not actually commit the crime and so should not be convicted. If he is a citizen, then he is innocent until convicted of a crime based on the evidence of that crime. Such a person might have the option of deportation, assuming that he can find some country that would take him with his record.

The right to secede requires not only allowing it, but the means to accomplish it. Currently our Second Amendment to bear arms is our means of secession. This means that to secede, one must forcibly revolt, and then win the war. Instead we are proposing that people have a peaceful means of seceding. They should be able to get on a bus and travel to the Federal Free Zone. If that zone is located around interstate highways, then getting to that zone would be easy enough for the poorest of citizen. And then they need to be afforded a place to stay also, or the option of leaving really is not an option. If they want to leave the country, then they should be provided a plane ticket to do so. Otherwise their only means of secession might be violence. By providing the means to secede, we can avoid a war of secession in any scale. This kind of freedom destroys the need to resort to violence to fix an issue. Of course the right to bear arms still is our guarantee of the right to secede, should the Federal Government ever withdraw that right.

The primary reason to deny the right to secede is that someone wants power over someone else, to take part of their wages from them. The Civil War was a clear violation of this right to secede. It resulted in forcing a group of people to come under the power of the rich Yankees, when they clearly thought that was oppression. On the other hand, while the South touted the right to Secede, it was removing that right from its black slaves, by the runaway laws.

Why did the powerful rich of the North want to hang onto the South? It was because they wanted its resources, which would give them more power. But if each worker owns his own home and keeps his full profit, then the rich of the North could not leverage the resources of the South for themselves. By the same token, the slaveholders wanted to hang onto the slaves because they were stealing the work profits of their slaves. Thus we see that the right to secession goes hand in hand with the right to keep the profit of your work, and is the essence of true freedom.

Under a Federal umbrella that guarantees each community the right to its own laws, secession becomes unnecessary, because there is absolutely no oppression, since everyone is getting the exact laws that they want. Also the desire to hold onto territory becomes mute, since no one is leveraging wealth from the work of others, and since each community is voluntarily supporting the Federal Government, as a means of working together to protect the rights and land of all the communities. It becomes a selfish desire of each community to contribute to that Federal Government whatever it needs to do that.

The right to secede also means that a citizen should have the right to start his own community, if no current community suits him. Perhaps land from the Federal Free Zone could be granted to make a new community. These Exclusive Communities will be efficiently compact, leaving a lot of left over land for the Federal Free Zone, and national parks. Conversely anytime a citizen left a community, a plot of land could be given back to the adjacent Federal Free Zone. This would allow a buffer for those with unusual ideas or values. But normal population growth needs to be handled by building up or down as we do today.

This brings up the question of how small can a community be and still be viable? Could a 100 people make a small partially self-sustaining community? If they were networked with other communities, they could. The smaller this number is, the more minorities can have access to this full freedom.

Also, how unusual can these values be? Well one limitation should be when those values hurt someone. For example if a community is polluting the water table that affects other communities, that should be addressed in the State or Federal Legislatures. So inter-community complaints would have be handled by suppressing the 'freedom' of one or both of the parties to some degree, as is currently authorized in the Federal Constitution.

But what about hurting someone inside of the community? If the adults are consenting, then they should have their freedom. The whole point of Exclusive Communities is so that people who do not think like you can be separated from you, so that they can do their own thing, and learn from their mistakes. And we know that they are consenting if they are doing something allowed by their community's laws, because if one did not like that law, he could move to another community.

But what about children? Do children really have a say in cases of abuse? If not, should the Federal Government be able to come into a community to decide what is abuse, and what is not? This is a slippery slope that has pros and cons on both sides. It might be good for the Federal Legislature to make exceptions in some cases. But these exceptions should take a Constitutional Amendment, since they are is violating the basic principle of Secession. Thus the exceptions could not be enacted without three quarters majority vote. That would limit the exceptions to really legitimate ones, and err on the side of freedom for the communities.

By granting other communities the right to do things that you disapprove of, you are guaranteeing your right to do things that they disapprove of. For example if you disagree with them on the way that children should be raised, by allowing them to do that their way, you are guaranteeing that they cannot restrict how you raise your children in any way.

And at the same time you are insulating your community from those things that they are doing. This means that they cannot get a hold of your children to do that to them through some government agency, or adoption, or any other means. In this sense they are a separate sovereign country, which is the actual definition of the word, 'State.'

This fundamental right to secede is the foundation of the concept of Exclusive Communities. Exclusive Communities under a Federal guarantee of freedom to make their own laws is the only model that truly allows any individual the means of avoiding oppression. This is the model that the Founding Fathers wanted to achieve. The divergence into the two party system was unintended by the Constitution and eventually derailed that goal. It is up to us to now right that wrong.

Disaster Readiness

Self-sustaining communities connected to a network of communities under a Federal umbrella are able to weather larger disasters. Our electric grid today makes us vulnerable to disasters. Iran currently has plans to detonate an Electro-Magnetic-Pulse (EMP) device above New York City that would fry anything electronic. This could cause a chain reaction shutting down a large portion of our grid. A large sun flare, like the one back in 1859 that fried telegraph lines, could do this across the entire world. Estimates are that such an event with our current system could shut down the entire grid for 6 months or more, and result in the deaths of two thirds of the population of the civilized world. Recently we have seen storms that have shut down large areas of the grid for weeks. If the storm was larger it could devastate larger areas. And global warming scenarios include much larger storms.

Our infrastructure is entirely dependent on electricity. If the electricity goes out, water cannot be pumped to you. Refrigeration goes out. Gas cannot be pumped to run generators. Cities have only a three days food supply. After that people will start starving in mass. But a self-sustaining community grows much of its own food. It has responsibility for its own survival and thus would have its own contingency plans, or alternative power systems. These communities could survive much larger disasters for longer times.

Self-sustaining communities just make sense, unless you are the superrich who can make a buck from disasters by providing products that are in high demand, to people who do not have those things stockpiled. Corporations that are only concerned with the Bottom Line are not going to spend extra on contingencies that might help the workers. Isn't this the real reason that our disaster preparedness is so low right now?

Work as a Virtue

In our culture work is not a virtue. We want to make as much money as we can so we can retire early. We want a job that leverages work from others, so that we can get a cut of the pay of many people. Those who do not get to the 'top,' as it is called, are considered failures. That 'top' is on the top of a pyramid scam that leverages money from the wages of those below. And we want to work as little as possible because most jobs are miserable.

In Communism, work is a virtue. But this is simply rhetoric to enslave the people to the State. The fact that they end up getting little in return for their work destroys the economy by destroying the real incentive to work. Thus while they preach that work is a virtue, everyone stops listening to that eventually and then the economy fails.

But when we are allowed to keep the full profit from our work and stealing from workers in the form of interest and rent are outlawed, then work becomes a true virtue. And when we are working to support our community of friends, work is a virtue. How much we produce becomes a measure of our worth to the community.

But because we are a community of friends that 'production' is not just economic production. Encouragement, and not polluting, and not being obnoxious, because we are working with like-minded people, are also ways that we contribute to the community. These intangibles are part of the production that we contribute to the community. These intangibles make the workplace enjoyable. Thus our purpose is not to work as little as possible, but do our fair share and then some. And because our work is profitable, we will tend to work more, but not being enslaved to some workaholic boss.

Entertainment is very important in our society because it is how we let off steam that builds up at work. We build up resentment at work because of the widespread theft of our wages, and because of the poor working conditions of the corporate model, and the cut-throat competition. If our work was enjoyable, entertainment would be less important. We would need less of it. And because entertaining one's self does not contribute to the community, it would be less fulfilling than work.

As a profitable worker we could even work part time and easily make enough money to survive. And we could have more time for entertainment. In fact we would probably take extra time for socializing with our community of friends. Socializing would be our primary entertainment. That extra time would also be funneled into inventions and exploration. And because we are a co-op that makes the rules for our jobs, we would engineer socializing into the job in various ways to make it more enjoyable. But because we want to produce an over abundance, which we would share with our community, we will want to work more and more effectively. Work will be a true virtue.

Farming
The virtue of work can be seen easily in farming. Farms are heavy polluters today, and yet I am suggesting that we have some kind of a farm in each community, so we can be more self-sustaining. Farms today follow a monoculture model, meaning that they grow a whole bunch of one kind of crop. Again this derives from the Corporate model, where the Bottom Line is the only important thing. When a pest or fungus gets into that crop, it goes through the entire crop. This means that the crop must have lots of pesticide, which creates more resistant bugs. It also needs lots of fertilizer because monoculture depletes the soil. And the pesticide and the fertilizer are what pollute the water table.

Organic farmers recognize this problem and use a multi-crop model. Thus when a pest gets in, it only damages one crop of many. Natural forms of pest control,

like ladybugs are used instead. This is not polluting.
Organic farming is nearly as profitable as monoculture
farming because it does not have pay for the huge amounts
of pesticide and fertilizer. A community that lives next to
a farm, and works there as a Co-op, will want a non-
polluting organic farm. This will cause monoculture farms
and their pollution to go away.

Organic farms are generally more work intensive.
Because of the huge cut stolen by interest and land
payments, the profit margin is very slim. In order to make
ends meet, they have to employ few people that work
extra hours for less pay. If the lion's share of the profits
were not stolen, they would be highly profitable.

The main thing that people need is food. As the
population grows, the need for food grows. It is
something that will always be in demand regardless of the
economy. If organic farmers kept their full profits, they
could have more people working the farm in order to
lower the hours required. But even so these farms are
enjoyable because the work directly produces profit. They
are enjoyable because the work is done with friends. They
are enjoyable because the environment is clean and
beautiful.

And the work is fulfilling because it is providing
something needed for other people. We have a need to
contribute to others hard wired inside us. Theft breaks us
by not allowing us to fulfill that need. And once broken,
we fall into depression, or break down altogether, or we
lash out with outbursts or violence. The answer to these
problems is not drugs or incarceration. The answer is
outlawing theft of wages and instituting Exclusive
Communities, so that we can fulfill our need to contribute
by the virtue of work.

But Exclusive Communities need not all be rural.
A community could inhabit a high-rise building. That one
building could house a non-polluting factory, residences,
shops and entertainment. The factory could be offices,

though there will be less demand for offices, as the corporate hierarchy no longer pays.

But a city building could be a farm too. It could use hydroponics. It could even use regular gardens, situated on the south side of the building. But in any case, communities will be built around something that provides real products or services, rather than some means of stealing money from other workers. This means more stuff to go around in the long run, making your income worth more in the marketplace.

The Federal Budget

Now that we understand the Profit Motive, Flat Tax, Innocent till proven guilty, and Exclusive Communities, we are prepared to take on the complicated topic of the Budget. These new ways of dealing with the economy will demand a new way of dealing with the Budget.

Those of us who are outside of the Budget arena, may think that each major unit of the government gets a percentage of the tax income. This is the way that pie charts are presented to the public. But if this were true, then there would never be deficit spending. If exactly 100% of the tax income was given out by percentages to all the agencies, then exactly 100% of the tax income would be spent; no more and no less. There would never be any leftovers, and there would never be any over expenditures. In fact I am proposing that we move to this type of Budget, so that deficit spending would be impossible.

Currently the way the system really works is that the peons in the trenches write up their own budgets. These are guys who may have a lot of knowledge of the Budget, or may be newly assigned to the task, having gotten little or no education on how the system works. They may not even know about some of the obligations made by their predecessors, that will later come in as unexpected bills. They have to put down dollar amounts for each project they want to do that year, and they have to write a justification for each one. They have to write in some bogus amounts so that they will have a slush fund for contingencies, since having an emergency fund is illegal. And many write in bogus amounts for bogus projects, so they can get illegal things, or give it to Corporations for the promise of an inflated job when they get out of the government. But some do not and then they have legitimate emergencies that may fall through the cracks.

This Budget Request is submitted to the Budget Office that assigns each unit to an employee, who took a course in budgeting and is now in charge of deciding how important night-vision goggles are for the Quartermaster Corps. So they flip a coin, based on what mood they are in that morning, and decide how much to cut; a little, the whole thing, or nothing. Usually they cut a little. So the guys who inflated their figures will get what they want, and the honest ones will be short.

In short, the guys in the trenches are writing their own budgets, while the ignorance of the watchdogs lets them get away with it. The amount of money they get is not based on how important their mission is to the voters, but on how much they ask for. Thus the guy down in supply who knows the system gets a huge plush office, while the infantry is freezing is substandard ponchos.

Next these figures are tallied up and submitted to Congress. Congress has to decide how much to cut each project, in dollar figures. This is based on political discussions. The projects that have the most lobbying get cut less. All of this is so complicated that the Congressmen have to employ Budget Analysts to do the work and make recommendations. Again the Budget Analyst knows nothing about night-vision goggles or Quartermasters when they make their recommendations.

But in the end they feel good about cutting that Supply Sergeant's budget from $50,000 to $40,000, not knowing that $40,000 will easily pay for his mahogany furniture and his golf lessons, which were justified as 'Quartermaster Supplies.' And then they wonder why the Federal Budget keeps going up each year, even though the tax revenues go down, because more people are doing Budget jobs instead of producing things.

Once the Budget is cut, the figures are distributed back to the trenches. The units must spend the entire amount in that year. So the guys that inflated will have leftovers. That money has to be spent that year, or it will be cut more the next year. So they spend it on junk they don't need, because they know they will need more money next year. Those who are frugal will have their budget cut more next year.

The Marine Corps used to pride itself on giving money back each year. Eventually they got their Budget cut so far back, that they literally did not even have bullets or gas. So they changed and got with the program, and are now spending extra on junk, just like everyone else. This is an example of how this evil Budget system converted a group that was trying to be moral and responsible into typical thieves of the public trust, to compete with everyone else it has corrupted.

So the solution that I am proposing is that Congress decides on percentages, rather than dollar amounts. Each major unit should get a percentage of the tax revenue, based on the importance of their mission politically. So if the representatives agree that Social Services should get 60% and the military get 40% or whatever, they are doing so because they believe that percentage reflects the relative importance of each service to our society. This makes the system transparent to the voters, so that changes can be made based on the voter's conscience, instead of Pork Barreling.

Then each unit will get a varying amount of money each year, based on how much taxes actually came in. Then it would be in their selfish interest to spend their money as efficiently as possible. The Commanders would be held accountable for their missions, rather than following complicated Budget rules. The better they budgeted to provide more firepower with the money they have, the better their Fitness Reports and promotions will be. Currently their Fitness Reports are downgraded for silly things like not spending the exact amount of projected money by artificial deadlines. It is better for their promotions if they spend money on junk to make the figures add up exactly.

To make this work, we would also need to get rid of the requirement to spend all the money in one year. That way they can keep some in reserve and budget normally like we budget our homes or businesses. Currently if a project costs more than projected, or if the money for the project is cut due to lack of tax revenues, the project often has to be scrapped after paying for a portion of it. Without the requirement to spend all the money at the end of the year, that project could simply be completed the following year. Contractors would not have their contracts torn up after buying the supplies. Nor would they have to sue the government to pay for the supplies, which it now no longer needs. Instead of a bunch of Budget Analysts and high paid managers working through the night to reallocate money from this pot to that before some artificial deadline, the time schedule for the project could simply be altered, and no deficit spending would be required.

Commanders could concentrate on doing their jobs better, instead spending all of their time on these artificial rules and trying to get around the Budget system. I remember going to Staff Meeting after Staff Meeting where training was brushed over or ignored because all the time was taken up by artificial budgeting issues. The Commander knew every detail of the Budget, but knew nothing of the fact that training was being cut over and over, because the officers were too busy with their Budget issues.

The amount of regulations that we have in the Budget arena is ridiculous. Each project is submitted to the Contracting Office who sits on it for months, trying to figure out all the red tape. The Contracting Office employees are graded on fitting the regulations exactly, not making the units better, or even for actually getting supplies to the units. They even get plus marks for kicking requests back for a technicality. Getting rid of the Civil

Courts will get rid of the frivolous lawsuits in this area, which are what drives the many of these regulations. Instead of regulations and inspections, we would have a relatively few laws about how to spend the money, with severe punishments to deter actual crime. And because the Commander's Fitness Report is tied to how efficiently he budgets for his mission, he will want to spend his money wisely, instead of on junk.

Many of these regulations deal with hiring minority companies, or giving government benefits in exchange for corporate favors. If the big corporations could not manipulate the market because of the other reforms we have discussed earlier, quality would truly drive the market. Commanders, graded on their 'bang for the buck,' would buy from the best quality Co-ops, rather than always choosing the cheapest bid, as is the current practice. But the cheapest bid, while guaranteeing the lowest quality, does not guarantee the cheapest price. Under our current system it is typical for companies to under bid to get a contract and then inflate the bill. The Budget Office pays on receipts, not bids. And thus the amount spent is normally much higher than the original budget projection, based on the phony bid. Therefore the budget is all over the map at the end of the year, and the quality is in the pits.

I remember one of my moves in the military, where the cheapest bidder was picked for the move. And true to form, they damaged a lot of my stuff. After the fact, they charged twice as much. Then the government docked my pay for the difference, because it was now over the budget ceiling, like it was my fault. Service members put up with these types of shenanigans all the time, and are not allowed to sue the government about it. The same Commander that authorized it, is the same guy that judges the complaint. The Corporation, that had some backdoor deal with a Contract Official, makes out like a bandit, and the little guy gets the shaft.

On the other hand, if the units simply bought locally from the new State they were operating in, then there would be no minorities, since each state is made of like-minded value groups. And since the workers keep the profits of their work and there are no corporations, the lobbying, bribing and general misbehavior will go away. We could reduce the Budget to simple considerations of quality, reliability, and efficiency, because that is what is in the best interest of the managers.

Another thing that will help the Budget is that Exclusive Communities will be responsible for more. They will take over the bulk of the social programs, cutting the Federal social Budget to practically nothing. Exclusive Communities will have a vested interest in taking care of their own social needs efficiently. They will thus provide better services for less, while the Federal Government will provide services only for the gaps in the coverage that are left. And these gaps will be provided for based simply on the percentage designated for each need according to the importance of each one, as decided by the voters.

The Military could be done in a similar way. Each community could be tasked with providing a squad of armed soldiers, or a jet with its crew, rather than extra taxes for the Government to do it for them. And they could provide the ammunition and supplies, whenever they were called on for maneuvers or war. This way the community or the State would regulate the budget for these units, rather than the Federal Government. As a community it would be in their interest to spend their money efficiently for this requirement. They would want their friends to have the best equipment to stay alive in war, and they would want to get them at the best prices so that they have more left over to spend on other things they need. The Federal Government might only provide certain special units, such nuclear missile units, or coordinators that would help the units work together by deciding on common ammunition calibers, etc. Thus its budget would require a lot less.

And by providing money based on percentages and letting the Commanders do their own budgets, they would get a bigger 'bang for the buck.' The Commanders would have to follow certain laws agreed to by Congress, but that would be much less complicated than the tons of regulations that currently require hiring teams of specialists to deal with. This would have the added benefit of freeing up those Budget Analyst positions, so those people can get back to actually producing goods or services, increasing the actual buying power of everyone, instead of being a drain on the Budget.

But think about these regulations. The Budget is regulated partly by laws from Congress, plus a whole bunch of regulations made by the Budget Office, which belongs to the Executive Branch. These regulations are in effect laws, but they are not made by Congress. They are made by the Executive Branch. Remember that only Congress can make laws according to the Constitution. Thus these are not Constitutional by definition. Again we need to get back to the Congress being the only Branch that makes laws. And because Congress will be based on value groups rather than Corporate Lobbyists, those laws will be equitable, rather than Pork Barrel.

By going to a percentage Budget rather than a dollar amount Budget, we would automatically get rid of deficit spending that adds to the total deficit each year. And then we could simply vote to give 5% of the revenues to pay off the accumulated national debt. By letting communities provide social and other services, the Federal Budget will be lowered and the community budgets will be handled much more efficiently and wisely. Commanders will be concerned with keeping their men alive in battle, rather than trying to somehow beat the convoluted Budget system. By making Commanders simply responsible for doing the best for their mission, it will be in their interest to manage their Budget efficiently, which was the original the intent of the regulations that don't work, because they add spending for dealing with the red tape. We will get the Budget out of the hands of Corporate Lobbyists, and into the hands of the communities and voters.

Druthers

Are you the type that wants to party all night, or do you want go to bed, so you can get up early for work? With Exclusive Communities both of you can have what you want. And you do not have to live next to each other and pound on each other's walls when you are trying to sleep.

Is your hobby bowling, or drag racing, or worship? Wouldn't you want to live in a community of like-minded people? If you are a bowling type, do you want to live next to a drag strip? And if you are a dragster type, do you want to live next to bowling alley? And when you go to the local hangout do you want it to be in a non-smoking place, or do you want to smoke there? With Exclusive Communities, everyone can have exactly what they want, and you can have neighbors that are into the same things and hours that you are. The political tug-of-war about each of these many lifestyle issues would be over, and we could all move in the direction that we want.

Of course there will be a down side. The people on welfare will have to work as part of their community, but they will find their lives more fulfilling. The rich will have to get a real job that does something besides stealing from the poor.

Everywhere you turn, Exclusive Communities will make our lives better. If we outlaw making money from our money, provide homes to citizens, get rid of civil courts and go to a flat tax, we will motivate the workers to work, because they can keep the profit from their work. Production and the economy will go up. Excusive Communities will allow us to live securely with like-minded people. Crime will go down. Disaster preparedness will go up. We can stop the political tug-of-war about lifestyle issues and get everything that we ever wanted politically without the huge outlay of money and effort for campaigns. We will all finally be able to really pursue life, liberty and happiness.

Summary:

1. Outlaw making money from money. This includes outlawing interest, rent, patents, and going to a flat tax. This requires changing all corporations into co-ops. This requires dissolving all mortgages and giving domiciles to those who live in them. This will allow workers to keep the profits of their work, by not allowing the rich to leverage their wealth to steal from the poor.

2. Fix our broken Justice system. Award compensation in criminal courts and dissolve civil courts. Return to the Constitution by outlawing Precedence Law. All ambiguities in the law should be returned to the Legislature for clarification. Innocent until proven guilty means no blanket searches, inspections, tests, or licenses for citizens. This will eliminate frivolous suits and restore a climate that encourages small businesses.

3. Facilitate Exclusive Communities by first making them legal. Encourage self-sustaining walking communities with tax options. Those that provide various social services could opt out of taxes for those Federal and State services. These communities that provide living space next to work, shops and amusement will naturally be non-polluting, supportive to neighbors and secure. They will naturally provide basic education so that all can help produce for the benefit of the whole. Each community would be made of like-minded people, which could enact laws independently, without different-minded people voting against what they want. In this way everyone can have exactly the laws that they want without the tug-of-war that is inherent in a multi-cultural democracy.

Transitioning

The economy of sharing that I am describing here is actually relatively simple. It is much less complicated than our current laws. The difficulty with it is in the transition from what we are currently doing, because it requires a lot of unlearning, and a complete change in the way we think. It is not that it is complicated, but that it is foreign to our current thinking. It is difficult for most people to switch gears. They are afraid of the unknown. And certainly such a large change will cause some amount of upheaval at best. But we have a choice to either change to do something different, or remain doing what we are doing, which is failing, and which will lead to a complete collapse of our society.

At this point, let's imagine how the transition might proceed. A large shift of cultural paradigm, which we are talking about would require a major transition plan. This transition should be gradual where ever that is possible.

Some of the new laws would have to be Constitutional Amendments because the Constitution was built on the economy of Laissez-Faire. There would have to be a national dialogue about this change. Those who recognize that our current paradigm is failing would have to unite to promote some kind of a complete change. We would have to see that we have a choice between complete change, or complete collapse.

Our Founding Fathers called America a 'great experiment.' The Pyramid on our Great Seal is unfinished, because it symbolized that our government experiment was not finished. They were experimenting with something completely different that would have to be changed in the future as the results of that experiment came in. They recognized that what countries had been trying in the past all failed, and that a complete paradigm shift was necessary. And as with all experiments, it is a process of trial and error.

We need to find a new solution that has not been tried. We need to understand the various solutions that have already failed, so that we can avoid them. Historically Laissez-Faire collapsed because of the greed of the rich, and Communism collapsed in reaction to the bare shelves. And middle of the road Socialism is currently collapsing as the two parties are locked in a perpetual tug-of-war, while greed tears us apart.

The details of the transition plan will depend on the agreements of the people. They must take into consideration the resources and geography of the territories, and the situations and druthers of the people involved. And thus the exact details cannot be anticipated. But the framework here will help us as we negotiate those details. Fairness and equity should be foremost in our discussions. We will have to get past our innate selfishness to reap cooperation as we go forward. We should all be happy as long as we compare the agreement to our alternative of a complete meltdown of society.

Does a complete meltdown sound a little paranoid? I will give you that. But I am a student of history. I have noticed that throughout history things will be going along relatively smoothly, if wholesale theft of the work profits of the majority can be called smoothly. But then at some point, the masses get fed up with the theft and revolt, and a bloodbath ensues. In many cases, it is a complete meltdown. Then people are ready to negotiate seriously. They are so ready that they accept someone else as a dictator. So a meltdown is not farfetched. It is an historical probability. And that will end up with a regime change, but the theft will continue until it melts down again. We have a choice to break out of that cycle of slaughter and tyranny. If we agree that our choice is change or meltdown, we can make the sacrifices necessary for the compromises required for a fair transition plan.

So we need to agree on a goal of a completely new experiment, and then on a transition plan that causes the least amount of upheaval. Obviously some upheaval is necessary, since the new paradigm requires some new institutions and the removal of some old institutions. But this can be done peacefully, if people do not try to hang onto the old system that is not working.

The Transition Plan

<u>I would start by charting the new States.</u> This will give people a sense of the home they are heading for. It will give them a sense of stability during the transition. And even though they are still spread across the country, they can start organizing and thinking like a community of like-minded people. To some degree they can even start assisting each other. Instead of dreading the disaster that we are currently sinking into, we would be getting excited about our coming freedom and prosperity.

A vote could take place where everyone identifies the values of the communities that they want to live in. Then caucuses of like-minded people could develop Constitutions for each value group. Then a final vote where each person chooses the Constitution that they want to fall under. Then States could be chosen based on value groups, or coalitions of small value groups. Then land for the new States and the Federal Free Zones could be distributed based on the populations of each group. Then each value group could organize themselves into communities in their own way, based on the structures and resources found in their territories, and the druthers of the members.

The constituents of these new States at this point will still be spread all over the country. But new congressional districts can be made based on the names of the constituents, rather than geography. This is how parliamentary governments are set up. The next elections should then represent the various value groups of the nation, as the Constitution intended. Once they finish moving into their territories, say ten years down the line, the value groups will once again be based on geographic areas, as they were with the original make up of the States.

<u>Next we could fix the judicial system.</u> This will provide a better small business climate. This will also reduce the amount of lawsuits, thus reducing prices.

Violent crime punishments would increase to mandatory execution for violent crimes, and fines for all others. Indenturing for paying fines would be instituted. Prisoners would serve out their previous sentences until the prisons were emptied. The empty prisons could be given away as domiciles for the homeless.

Outlaw Precedent Law and the suppression of evidence, and return to the separation of the Legislative Branch of government as the Constitution requires. Any time a case cannot be decided, because the law is indistinct, it would be referred back to the Legislature to clarify the law.

Empower the Criminal Courts to award compensation for the victims at several times the amount of the damage as a deterrent. Change Civil Courts into Criminal Courts. Initially there will be more criminal cases because all crimes will have to be tried. Currently many minor cases are never tried, because our courts are overloaded. These ignored cases can be taken care of them in the converted Criminal Courts, instead of the Civil Courts. Thus justice will be extended to all victims through our Criminal Courts, not just to those that can afford to pay lawyers for civil cases. Gradually as work profits are restored to the workers and people move into secure like-minded communities, crime will take a nose dive. Then we will start cutting the amount of Courts and the amount of tax dollars we have to spend on them, which will help our deficit problem.

Setting up the new States and fixing the Judicial system will get us back to the intent of the Constitution, which is Representative Government and the separation of the branches of the Government. The next changes will fix the problem of the rich stealing the profits of the workers.

Then incrementally outlaw stealing work profits. This will allow the workers to keep their full profits from their work. This should boost the buying power of the workers, and thus stimulate the economy. This should also motivate some non-workers to get back to work. And those who have been making a living by stealing income from workers will move into jobs that actually produce goods or services, rather than taking a cut from the economy, as the lending institutions diminish.

Interest could be lowered incrementally over time till it was outlawed altogether, except for foreign loans. In Scripture, interest to foreigners is allowed because we are competing with them. While we want our neighbors to succeed, foreigners are those that are opposed to our way of life. So the fact that they need to borrow from us at interest, is a peaceful way of conquering their bad ideas. Success in the foreign market then is a peaceful means of showing which system works best.

Mortgages could be dissolved incrementally over a number of years. At the same time rent could be reduced in a corresponding manner, until all domiciles belong fully to their occupants. Bank owned homes will be given to homeless veterans. These changes should be done using bankruptcy controls, because the banks will be reduced to a small fraction of what they were.

Current Patents and Copyrights could first revert to the creators completely, and their time period could be reduced to say fifteen years. And at the same time we would cease to make new ones.

Changing over to a flat tax could be done at a particular year in the future, so that people could plan their taxes.

Then convert Corporations to Co-ops. This will give full profits to the workers, and get workers back to work. It will also motivate the former stockholders to get back to contributing to the economy. They will need to produce things or services, instead of taking a cut from the economy.

Bankruptcy procedures should also be used here to make the transition, so that the management does not funnel company funds into their pockets. The company would retain funds for operating and pensions. U.S. portions of foreign Corporations could be traded for those portions of U.S. corporations that are on foreign soil. Shareholders should be given the option to work at the company, or lose a portion of their shares. Those companies that have a surplus of funds beyond that can pay portions to former shareholders. Each worker would be given a portion of the company and then elect a new board. That new board would determine how to share the profits.

These new laws concerning stealing, co-ops and justice should increase work and production. New businesses should start up because of a more supportive justice climate. This would increase the economy and the tax revenues, so we can bailout Social Security and fix the deficit.

Those who are on government or company pensions or Social Security or disability should have those payments guaranteed by the government until they join a community of their choice. Once a community takes over their care, that community could opt out of the taxes for Social Security, Medicare and other social services.

Those who are depending on mutual funds for retirement will lose that source of income, though as former shareholders they have the option of becoming a worker at one of the Co-ops to keep their shares. They will also have Social Security and they will have their mortgages dissolved. State and Private nursing homes will need to remain open during the transition. Thus they will be able to survive until they move into a community.

Exclusive Communities will need to take care of the elderly, by both providing for their needs, and employing them in part-time jobs that they can handle. In this way most will become contributing members of the community.

Those that are too ill to work at all will be guaranteed to be able to join the community of their choice by the transition voting process discussed above. In this way the communities will take on the obligation to take care of the infirmed and disabled, once they have relocated and are operational.

Communities can take care of them at a level above Social Security because the community also provides the intangibles like exercise and friends beyond just money. And as they join communities, and production increases, tax revenue will increase, and the people being paid by the government will decrease to manageable numbers.

Once that is accomplished, people will naturally want to move into their new communities of like-minded people. This is where we can start a slow transition to Exclusive Communities and new States. Because the transition will require people to change jobs, it needs to be done gradually. But because the workers will be getting their full personal profits, they will relatively quickly be able to save up plenty to fund these new communities.

A National Register of Communities could be enacted, where the communities could advertise their constitutions, vacancies, products and contact information. Anyone who wanted to move into a community could use the register to find people willing to trade domiciles. This could be done by first moving into the Federal Free Zone and then applying to move into the community of your choice, or by a multi-way trade, or by moving into vacant apartments. Then we can start getting to know our new like-minded neighbors, and building and enjoying our new utopias.

Jumpstarting the Economy

The economic stalemate will be jumpstarted by the change in worker climate and friends helping friends in communities.

What stalls an economy? It is not the lack of materials or workers. Nor is it even the lack of money, since there are rich people with wads of it. It is the disconnect between workers and their profit.

An economic stall requires first a bad worker climate, where the rich are stealing too much of the profits of the workers. If the worker cannot start a business of his own because of the culture of lawsuits, he stops working. Or if he gets fed up with the amount of profit being stolen from him and goes on welfare or into crime. Or if he retires early, or has a breakdown, because the workplace is too miserable. Or a worker gets laid off by a greedy corporation that wants to hire cheaper labor.

On top of this add a few unexpected disasters. If a worker gets sick and goes on disability, or if there is a natural disaster, or a drought, or a disaster caused by shoddy safety procedures, because a corporation is trying cut costs for the Bottom Line.

All of these things separate a worker from his profit. And if this happens to a lot of people all at once, on top of a bad worker climate, the economy stalls, because there are suddenly a lot of people not buying things.

That is a show-stopper in an economy that is made of Corporations whose only concern is the Bottom Line. They will only produce things for a profit. Instead of continuing to produce things and giving them away and losing money to get the economy going again, they stop producing, lay off more people, and hope the prices will go up. They have to do this or they will lose their shareholders. Well the prices go up, but there is no one who is buying, so everything grinds to a halt.

In our transition plan, we started with changing the laws. By converting to co-ops, outlawing interest, giving domiciles to those who live in them, workers will be motivated to get back to work because they will suddenly own their full profits. And changing our judicial system to support small business startups will get others back to work. We will be producing things in hopes of eventually selling them and thus the economy can start moving.

Then by putting people in communities, they can work and share with their new friends, allowing the recipients to have more, so they can start buying things. This can work prior to moving into the new place for the community to some degree, by new friends in the value groups helping new friends, long distance.

In an Exclusive Community of people who work to help each other possess food, shelter and clothing, the lack of an economy becomes less of a concern. The workers who possess the basic necessities of a home and a co-op job only need to buy food and medicine in the short run to survive. And part of their food will be produced by their friends and shared with them for services. Thus they do not need a huge income. So while the products that they are making may not be selling for much, it will be enough to survive on. This means that the economy can start moving and will increase the opportunity for profit from work. It is only when a large portion of his profit is stolen that he has to make a huge profit to survive. An Exclusive Community insures that the worker can keep working, and eventually profit fully from that work and get the economy going, while surviving relatively comfortably in the mean time.

Our Choice

People have to get back to work for the economy to start working again. Continuing to do what we are doing, throwing money at the problem and the political tug of war will lead to revolts, chaos and bloodbaths, as recent growing unrest indicates. So staying in your comfort zone, sponging off the work of others, indefinitely is not an option. If we compare these major paradigm changes with simply staying in our comfort zone, they seem radical and scary. But if they are compared to the inevitable chaos that will result from doing nothing different, then radical change suddenly seems prudent.

In the thirties we got back to work by government projects, which is simply a mild form of Communism. This did not work very well evidenced by the fact that the country remained in the depression for ten years until WWII. It did not work because it required taking all the profits of the workers by taxes to pay for the projects, since the government is so inept, compared to a free market.

On the other hand, WWII worked because people were working to protect the country. They were working double hours for less pay out of patriotism, a form of community teamwork. The problem with jumpstarting the economy with a war is that a lot of people get killed in the process. On the other hand communities also get people working with little pay initially, but without the destruction and killing of war.

Another option, which is the direction we are heading, is for the rich to enslave the poor completely under a police state. This is done by encouraging fear. Sound familiar? This devolves into a Communist state, where the slaves lose their motivation to work, starve because of the bare shelves, or eventually revolt.

Which option do you like?

Conclusion

The only group of people that stand to lose from this Exclusive Community idea are the superrich. Self sustaining communities buy less goods from the conglomerates. But more than that, communities that are united are not propagandized by the superrich as easily. So the billionaires will have to survive on mere millions, and get a job that does not involve the theft of the wages of others; kind of like the rest of us, except we don't have the millions.

The superrich have used propaganda to make our system of theft from the workers, seem like a good thing. This gets the workers to keep working, without noticing that most of their profits are being stolen.

But propaganda only works if you can keep the opposition divided and fighting amongst themselves. If the opposition gets together, and organizes, and starts thinking for itself, it will realize that the rich are stealing from them with a pyramid scam, and that they have an alternative, and that they have the power to implement it.

The rich can only keep us at bay if the soldiers and supporters do what they are told. But those soldiers and supporters are the workers that are exploited by the rich. They should be on the side of the workers, not the rich.

We are being oppressed by the superrich who are stealing 90% of our income. And the 'Occupy Wall Street' movement is the beginning of our recognition of that oppression.

The Declaration of Independence discusses what Americans should do about oppression.

"We hold these truths to be self-evident, that all men are created equal, that they are endowed by their Creator with certain unalienable Rights, that among these are Life, Liberty and the pursuit of Happiness.--That to secure these rights, Governments are instituted among Men, deriving their just powers from the consent of the governed, That whenever any Form of Government becomes destructive of these ends, it is the Right of the People to alter or to abolish it, and to institute new Government, laying its foundation on such principles and organizing its powers in such form, as to them shall seem most likely to affect their Safety and Happiness."

"Prudence, indeed, will dictate that Governments long established should not be changed for light and transient causes; and accordingly all experience hath shewn, that mankind are more disposed to suffer, while evils are sufferable, than to right themselves by abolishing the forms to which they are accustomed. But when a long train of abuses and usurpations, pursuing invariably the same Object evinces a design to reduce them under absolute Despotism, it is their right, it is their duty, to throw off such Government, and to provide new Guards for their future security."

Also by the Author:

Yeshua's Path

What did Yeshua (Jesus) teach His disciples? How did He transform this bunch of country bumpkins from Galilee into powerful apostles? Can we today duplicate His discipling course? 85 steps are laid out in Scriptural order, to take us from doing our own thing, to becoming God's trusted servants.

www.createspace.com/3517502
(Vol. 1)   ISBN-13: 978-1456421434

Derek Netsarim Yisrael (Path of Nazarene Israel):
Website:
groups.yahoo.com/group/CongregationOnTheWeb
Email: Eli144000@hotmail.com